The Catholic Church in State Politics

The Catholic Church in State Politics

Negotiating Prophetic Demands and Political Realities

David Yamane

A SHEED & WARD BOOK

ROWMAN & LITTLEFIELD PUBLISHERS, INC.
Lanham • Boulder • New York • Toronto • Oxford

A SHEED & WARD BOOK

ROWMAN & LITTLEFIELD PUBLISHERS, INC.

Published in the United States of America
by Rowman & Littlefield Publishers, Inc.
A wholly owned subsidiary of The Rowman & Littlefield Publishing Group, Inc.
4501 Forbes Boulevard, Suite 200, Lanham, Maryland 20706
www.rowmanlittlefield.com

PO Box 317
Oxford
OX2 9RU, UK

British Library Cataloguing in Publication Information Available

Library of Congress Cataloging-in-Publication Data

Yamane, David.
  The Catholic Church in state politics : negotiating prophetic demands and political
realities / David Yamane.
     p. cm.
  Includes bibliographical references and index.
  ISBN 0-7425-3230-5 (cloth : alk. paper) — ISBN 0-7425-3229-1 (pbk. : alk. paper)
  1. Catholic Church—United States—Political activity. 2. Church and state—United
States. I. Title.
  BX1407.P63.Y36 2005
  261.7'088'28273—dc22   2005009609

Printed in the United States of America

∞™ The paper used in this publication meets the minimum requirements of
American National Standard for Information Sciences—Permanence of Paper
for Printed Library Materials, ANSI/NISO Z39.48-1992.

For Paul, Hannah, and Mark

Contents

Acknowledgments

Although this book is not a revision of my dissertation, which focused on religious advocacy in Wisconsin, some of that research necessarily made its way into this project. I gratefully acknowledge, therefore, early grants from the Society for the Scientific Study of Religion and the Louisville Institute for the Study of American Religion. The encouragement and support of Mark Chaves, Robert Booth Fowler, and Gerald Marwell were crucial in the wake of the death of my dissertation advisor, Richard Schoenherr, as I was embarking on my dissertation research.

Many of the ideas presented here had their genesis in fruitful dialogues with my colleagues in the Pew Seminar on "Culture, Morality, and the Power of Religion in Social Life" at Calvin College in the summer of 2001. I am particularly grateful to the seminar's fearless leader, Christian Smith, who showed me the importance of seeing the glass as half full rather than half empty when it comes to the power of religion in social life.

The bulk of the writing of this book was completed while I was a postdoctoral fellow at the Pew-funded Center on Religion and Democracy at the University of Virginia in 2002–2003. James Davison Hunter, Joe Davis, Steve Jones, Brad Wilcox, Chuck Mathewes, Nicole Martin, and everyone associated with the Center did much to make my time in Charlottesville both joyful and fruitful.

This book could not have been written strictly on the basis of the public record. The cooperation and support of state Catholic conference directors—in completing my survey, providing written material, subjecting themselves to interviews, and reading drafts of chapters—was vital to the project's success. Dick Dowling of Maryland, John Huebscher of Wisconsin, and Mike McCarron of Florida were particularly supportive of this work.

Several students at the University of Notre Dame had a hand in the research on which this book is based. It's been my pleasure to know and work with Booker Graves, Andy Troeger, Amy Warner, Annika Brophy, and Buzz J. Smith.

It has been a pleasure to work with several individuals at Rowman & Littlefield / Sheed & Ward, including: executive editor Jeremy Langford, assistant editor Katie Lane, and production editor Marian Haggard. I also gratefully acknowledge those working behind the scenes at the press whose names I do not know but whose work I appreciate greatly.

Finally, special thanks are due to "Iron" John Bartkowski for pumping me up and spotting me when I was reaching the point of failure in the heavy lifting that producing a book involves. The examples he and Brad Wilcox set not only make me want to be a better scholar, but also—and more importantly—a better person.

This book is dedicated to my three children—Paul, Hannah, and Mark—who unknowingly made innumerable sacrifices over the years it took to research and write. May God bless you and keep you always.

Introduction

The Governor and the Archbishop

In August 1995, after nearly a decade of state tinkering with various welfare reforms, Wisconsin Governor Tommy G. Thompson introduced a comprehensive plan known as "Wisconsin Works" or "W-2," which would, to borrow Bill Clinton's 1992 presidential campaign mantra, "end welfare as we know it."[1] The Wisconsin State Assembly passed the plan by a margin of 73 to 25, the state senate concurred by a similarly wide margin (27 to 6) in March 1996, and the governor signed the bill into law that April. By now, the provisions of this variety of welfare reform are familiar, but at the time they were a radical departure from the existing policy. The nonpartisan Wisconsin State Legislative Reference Bureau summarized the main thrust of the plan as follows: "W-2 ends the 'entitlement' aspect of AFDC assistance. Participants will no longer be automatically granted cash payments and health care because they fit into certain categories and meet prescribed requirements. In general, their participation is limited to an overall total of 60 months, consecutive or nonconsecutive, and they will be expected to work. . . . Although W-2 services or benefits will depend on compliance with work requirements, W-2 participants have no guarantee that work will be available to them."[2] Given these provisions, when fully implemented, W-2 would have dramatic consequences for the lives of those it touched.

Among the most consistent and outspoken critics of certain aspects of W-2 was the hierarchy of the Catholic Church. Wisconsin's Catholic bishops responded to the governor's welfare reform plan—which

1

they had anticipated—by issuing a 12-page statement, *Reforming Welfare by Valuing Families*, and holding a press conference in the heart of Milwaukee's inner city to publicize the statement.[3] As the title of their statement suggests, the bishops called for welfare reform to be guided by certain fundamental values, particularly the value of family, but more fundamentally the sacredness of human life and the inherent dignity of the human person. Among their specific arguments were that "calls for affirming personal responsibility must not become a signal to abandon the poor. Nor must the desire to foster responsibility rationalize decisions by the community to deny or withdraw its support from the needy when social and economic conditions prevent a poor person or family from being self-sufficient." And, "Welfare reform should include policies that affirm and support commitment and marriage for parents of poor children. Such support is preferable to punitive approaches that, though motivated by a well-intentioned desire to discourage illegitimacy, have the effect of denying assistance to poor women and children." The statement concluded, "Welfare reform that is purely pragmatic, based only on reducing costs, and that is conceived in isolation from the needed values of our whole society will not be fruitful." Subsequently, the bishops' public policy arm, the Wisconsin Catholic Conference, was actively involved in the debates over W-2 in the legislature.

The most dramatic direct conflict between the governor and the church, however, came in the summer of 1996 when Wisconsin was seeking the federal waivers necessary to implement the program. Although the W-2 legislation had already been signed into law in Wisconsin, this administrative process gave opponents another opportunity to challenge aspects of the program they deemed harmful and unfair. The debate had significance beyond Wisconsin because W-2 style reforms were gaining favor in the Clinton administration and at the federal level generally. So, Milwaukee archbishop Rembert Weakland—well-known for his involvement in the United States Catholic Conference's 1986 pastoral letter on the economy, *Economic Justice for All*—wrote an editorial published in the *Washington Post* calling W-2's failure to protect children and its repeal of the "safety net" for the poor "not morally justifiable."[4] In response, at a public news conference, Governor Thompson demeaned the archbishop, calling him "Weakling" (rather than Weakland) and suggesting that he "should apologize to the people of the state of Wisconsin." Thompson's most widely quoted line mocked Weakland by reference to the fact that the archbishop was completing his dissertation on Ambrosian chant at Columbia University. The governor declared to the assembled media, *"The archbishop should come back to Wisconsin and read his Bible instead of playing the piano in New York."*

This face-off between the governor and the archbishop caused quite a stir in Wisconsin and provoked a range of public responses. For some observers, it was an example of religion overstepping its bounds to become involved in the secular world of politics. In a letter to the editor in Madison's *Capital Times*, Douglas Schewe maintained, "I believe Milwaukee Archbishop Rembert Weakland is out of line using the prestige and title of his office to write the *Washington Post* on a public issue." An editorial in Madison's *Wisconsin State Journal* maintained, "On this issue, the Catholic Church in Wisconsin has clearly moved beyond its mission—and duty—to speak out on moral concerns. The church has taken a political role in this debate, with representatives of the Wisconsin Catholic Conference issuing position papers, writing newspaper opinion columns, and engaging in what appears to be old-fashioned lobbying."[5]

Others found Thompson's criticism of the Catholic archbishop of Milwaukee out of line. The *Sheboygan Press* editorialized, "We would hope the governor would confine his remarks to a reasoned response on the issues and leave Bible interpretation to the clergy." State senate majority leader and Democrat Chuck Chvala called Republican Governor Thompson's demand that Weakland apologize "outrageous" and charged that he had reached "a new level of arrogance" in criticizing Weakland for standing up for the poor. An unsigned editorial in the *Capital Times* compared Thompson to England's King Henry II, who said of Thomas Becket, archbishop of Canterbury, "Who will free me from this turbulent priest?" The editorial reminded readers that Becket was soon murdered by King Henry's knights and concluded, "When a moral leader steps forward to remind the governor of his duties, Thompson resorts to insults. We are thankful that Tommy Thompson does not have the authority his predecessors did to silence a critic. But we could not help but hear the regal echo of King Henry II in our governor's pronouncements of recent days."[6]

A third view was that the whole episode was surreal or silly, if not both. And there is evidence to support this view. One newspaper characterized the governor as turning "into an unguided missile when the talk on welfare became biblical." A reporter at the news conference asked Thompson, "Wasn't Jesus a socialist?" to which Thompson responded, "I thought he was a free enterpriser. He was a carpenter's son and I thought he was doing well. He was able to change water into wine. Now that to me is the classic definition of a guy in the entrepreneurial spirit."[7]

The moral of this story goes beyond each of these overly simplistic interpretations. Each of these interpretations effectively seeks to negate the dynamic conflict that occurs when religion and politics meet: by disallowing religious critiques of politics and political criticisms of religion, or by trivializing the matter. But the issue is not simply that the archbishop as a religious authority or the governor as a political authority overstepped his bounds, or that the event is just comical. Rather than treating the episode as an aberration or something to be overcome, the conflict between the governor and the archbishop is best seen as "business as usual" when religion enters the public sphere in modern society. Thus understood, the conflict opens up to an important theoretical debate in the social scientific study of religion—the question of *secularization*—and focuses attention on an important but understudied empirical phenomenon—the *role of the Catholic Church in state-level politics*. This theoretical concern and empirical focus animate this book.

THEORETICAL CONCERN:
THE DOUBLE-MOVEMENT OF SECULARIZATION

This work, like all social scientific theorizing and research, is based on a pre-scientific intuition that I have tried to systematize and build upon in the course of my study. It is an intuition I share with many sociologists from the classical period forward and that can best be summarized by reference to a panel discussion on secularization at an academic conference recounted by sociologist Mark Chaves: "On the panel were Peter Berger, a long-time proponent of the classical secularization thesis, and Andrew Greeley, a long-time critic of secularization theses in any form. After a series of exchanges in which Professor Greeley debunked every claim and piece of evidence presented by Professor Berger in favor of the secularization thesis, Peter

Berger is said to have exclaimed, 'But Andy, *something* must have changed!'" My intuition is with Berger here, that something about the role of religion in society has changed. But what? Recalling the conflict between Governor Thompson and Archbishop Weakland over W-2 suggests one answer. It suggests that Chaves is fundamentally correct when he argues, "We may not live in a society with less religion. I suspect we never will. But we do live in a society with less *religious authority*. That, Peter Berger might have said to Andrew Greeley, is what has changed."[8]

The governor—a practicing Catholic who attended Mass at my parish in Madison regularly during this time—could chastise the Catholic archbishop in his state at a press conference, but could not have him killed. And the archbishop could criticize the governor in a major newspaper, but could not have him deposed. This exemplifies the differentiation of secular from religious authorities in modern societies. Our social structure, and in particular our polity, is *secularized* in this respect. That "institutional differentiation" in this sense is fundamental to secularization theory has been forcefully argued of late by a number of scholars.[9]

What is meant by institutional differentiation? According to sociologists Roy Wallis and Steve Bruce, in the course of modernization, "specialized institutions develop or arise to handle specific features or functions previously embodied in, or carried out by, one institution." As a consequence, in a highly differentiated society, the norms, values, and practices of the religious sphere have only an indirect influence on other spheres such as business, politics, leisure, and education. In Jose Casanova's excellent summary, he says, "the core and central thesis of the theory of secularization is the conceptualization of the process of societal modernization as a process of institutional differentiation and emancipation of secular spheres—primarily the state, the economy, and science—from the religious sphere." Consequently, "the primary 'public' institutions (state, economy) no longer need or are interested in maintaining a sacred cosmos or a public religious worldview." According to political scientist Donald Smith, "The secularization of the polity has been the most fundamental structural and ideological change in the process of political development."[10]

Unfortunately, some observers jump too quickly from this core thesis of secularization to a corollary that sees religion not only as differentiated from the secular sphere but also as wholly privatized. But one can, for example, recognize the differentiation of religious institutions and authorities from political institutions and authorities without requiring that religion and politics never interact. Secularization as differentiation simply means that when religion and politics meet, they do so under particular social structural conditions. Wolfgang Schluchter notes that "the de-politicization of religion as a result of functional differentiation does not mean, of course, that religious associations forgo politics." But, he continues, under these secularized conditions, religion "can at best be politically relevant but no longer politically dominant."[11] Casanova fundamentally agrees: institutional differentiation is "the unassailable core of modern theories of secularization," but the *privatization* of religion—the relegation of religion to the private sphere—is "a historical optional, a 'preferred option' to be sure, but an option nonetheless." And when religion plays a public role, it does so in a limited way:

> In modern differentiated societies it is both unlikely and undesirable that religion should again play the role of systemic normative integration. But by crossing boundaries, by raising questions publicly about the autonomous pretensions of the differentiated spheres to function without regard to moral norms or human considerations, public religions may help to mobilize people against such pretensions, they may contribute to a redrawing of the boundaries, or, at the very least, they may force or contribute to a public debate about such issues. Irrespective of the outcome or the historical impact of such a debate, religions will have played an important public role.[12]

Thus, to highlight the decline in the scope of religious authority is to tell only part of the story of the place of religion in modern society. Secularization does not simply *constrain* religious activity in politics and other differentiated societal spheres. Secularization also *enables* religious activity. I call this dual nature of secularization as both constraining and enabling the *double-movement* of secularization.[13] The *first moment* of this double-movement focuses not on the decline of religion, per se, but on the broad movement in the history of the West toward a decline in the scope of religious authority vis-à-vis secular authorities in the process of institutional differentiation. And the *second moment* recognizes the re-emergence of religious organizations in the political sphere, but under the secularized conditions established in the first moment. Put more concretely, under conditions of societal-level secularization, where the scope of religious authority over institutions such as courts and legislatures has diminished, religious groups that seek to be effectively involved in those institutions are constrained to work in ways that articulate with and are accommodative of the reality of a secular society.

Again, secularization does not mean that religion has no public role. It only means that public religion is constrained by the secularity of the modern, democratic political institutions. The challenge, then, is not to ask *whether* religion matters in public life, for clearly it does; rather, the challenge is to understand *how, when, and why* religion matters. This is a major task of the present study.

EMPIRICAL FOCUS:
THE CATHOLIC CHURCH IN STATE POLITICS

This theoretical perspective is brought to bear in an empirical study of the political advocacy of state Catholic conferences, the public policy arms of America's Catholic bishops at the state level. The focus on state Catholic conferences—rather than the better-known United States Conference of Catholic Bishops—is motivated by two important trends that emerged in late-twentieth-century America: the movement of the Catholic Church closer to the center of American political and social life, and the devolution of responsibility for policy making on many crucial issues from the federal government to the states.

Catholics in the Public Square

This project is motivated in part by the belief that the Catholic Church's political advocacy contributes to American democracy. That these once seemingly incompatible historical movements, Catholicism and democracy, can be spoken of at once represents a sea change both in American intellectual culture and in the place of Catholicism in American society. For much of the history of the modern West, the notion that religion could make a positive contribution to public life was suspect, particularly among Enlightenment *philosophes*. According to historian Crane Brinton, "The [philosophers of the Enlightenment], could they have been polled in the modern way, would probably have ranked the Roman Catholic church . . . as the greatest single corrupting influence" in society.[14] As the dominant church in France at the time of the Revolution, the Catholic Church was especially suspect among democrats. The fact that the British colonies were largely populated by adherents of Protestant confessions fleeing religious persecution in Europe and that the United States was subsequently established as a nation-state on Enlightenment principles helped to weave anti-Catholic sentiments deeply into the fabric of American thought and culture.

According to historian John McGreevy, the terms of mid-twentieth-century American liberalism "included the insistence that religion, as an entirely private matter, must be separated from the state, that religious loyalties must not threaten national unity, and that only an emphasis on individual autonomy, thinking on one's own, would sustain American democracy." The great enemy of this "democratic faith," as Arthur Schlesinger called it, was Roman Catholicism. Paul Blanshard's *American Freedom and Catholic Power* (1949)—a best seller and a Book-of-the-Month Club recommendation—was the most prominent example of this common sentiment. In a 1951 review of Blanshard's *Communism, Democracy, and Catholic Power*, the historian Perry Miller concluded "that Catholicism was antagonistic to both 'a free and critical education' and 'the democratic way of life.'"[15] Thus, well into the twentieth century, it would seem odd to many to speak of a Catholic "contribution" to democracy in America, for the church in its very nature was undemocratic and cultivated in its members undemocratic tendencies.

Much has changed since then. A unique concatenation of circumstances gaining strength in the 1960s resulted in the movement of the Catholic Church closer to the center of American political life than it had ever been historically. This included increasing social mobility and "Americanization" of individual Catholics and the *aggiornamento* (opening up to the world and internal updating) effected by the Second Vatican Council. Just one year after the close of the Council, Catholic priest and sociologist Andrew Greeley characterized it as "the Church's definitive break with the styles and patterns of behavior of a feudal and renaissance world and its assumption of the styles and patterns of behavior of the modern world." Later, Catholic theologian George Weigel (among others) offered a similar interpretation, focusing in particular on the key role played by the Vatican II "Declaration on Religious Freedom" (*Dignitatis Humanae*) in transforming the Catholic Church "from a traditional defender of the *ancien regime* into perhaps the world's foremost institutional defender of basic human rights."[16]

Taken together, these changes conspired to create what Richard John Neuhaus called a "Catholic Moment" in American history. Because of its sheer size, its unique and vital tradition of social thought, and the historic leadership of Pope John Paul II, "This can and should . . . be the moment in which the Roman Catholic Church in the United States assumes its rightful role in the culture-forming task of constructing a religiously-informed public philosophy for the American experiment in ordered liberty."[17] For many, this potential began to be realized in the 1980s with the publication of two pastoral letters by the U.S. bishops conference. Although they were not universally hailed, either within the church or without, *The Challenge of Peace: God's Promise and Our Response* (1983) and *Economic Justice for All* (1986) solidified the church's new position as an important voice in American public discourse. Internationally, the role of Pope John Paul II and the Catholic Church in the fall of communism in the Soviet Bloc reinforced the idea that the church could be an important ally of democracy.[18] As political scientist Richard Gelm has written about the situation in the United States, "Through the unprecedented activism of the National Conference of Catholic Bishops during the 1980s, American Catholic bishops assumed a position as chief religious commentators on American politics."[19] Although few seem to have noticed, the same is true in those states in which the bishops have been politically active.

The New Federalism

The second key trend in recent American history that motivates this study of state Catholic conferences is the devolution of responsibility for creating and implementing public policy from the federal government to the states. Under America's federal system of government, the states have always had considerable responsibility for creating and implementing public policy. They have not always received much respect for their ability to handle that responsibility. We have, therefore, come a long way from the English observer James Bryce's famous quip in *The American Commonwealth* (1906) that "the state legislatures are not high-toned bodies" to political scientist Carl Van Horn's more recent assessment that state governments "are arguably the most responsive, innovative, and effective level of government in the American federal system."[20]

According to political scientist David Hedge, "America is in the midst of a 'devolution revolution' as increasing amounts of responsibility for governing the nation are shifted to the American states."[21] Ushered in by Jimmy Carter and Ronald Reagan, continued by George H. W. Bush and Bill Clinton, and bolstered by the Republican congressional and gubernatorial "landslide" of 1994, this rebalancing of the rights and responsibilities of the federal and state governments, known as the "New Federalism," promises to make state government an even more vital arena for students of American politics and policy in the future.

The "devolution" to the states of responsibility for such policy matters as abortion and welfare is well underway. The Supreme Court's decision in *Webster v. Reproductive Health Services* (109 S. Ct. 3040 [1989]) in large part shifted responsibility for the regulation of abortion back to the states, which in the 16 years following *Roe v. Wade* (410 U.S. 113 [1973]) had little to say outside of funding issues. The 1992 Supreme Court decision in *Planned Parenthood of Southeastern Pennsylvania v. Casey* (91-744) reaffirmed *Webster*, allowing states to pass laws restricting abortion so long as no "undue burden" was imposed. According to political scientists Michael Berkman and Robert O'Connor, "Responding to the *Webster* decision, state legislators introduced over 400 abortion-related bills in the 40 state legislatures that were still in session in July 1989 [when the decision was handed down] or met in 1990."[22] Clearly, state legislatures are taking the devolution of authority on abortion policy quite seriously.

Another significant moment for devolution was when Congress passed and President Clinton signed the Personal Responsibility and Work Opportunity Reconciliation Act (PRWORA) of 1996 (P.L. 104–193). Like the "Wisconsin Works" (W-2) program on which it was modeled, PRWORA reformed welfare by eliminating the open-ended entitlement to Aid to Families with Dependent Children (AFDC) and replacing it with a Temporary Assistance to Needy Families (TANF) block grant for states to provide time-limited cash assistance for needy families, with work requirements for most recipients. States may use their TANF funding in any manner "reasonably calculated to accomplish the purposes of TANF."

With the possible exception of war, over which states have little control, most of the issues of concern to religious advocacy organizations are being addressed in some fashion at the state level. This includes, of course, abortion and welfare reform, but important policy decisions are also being made on capital punishment, school reform, same sex marriage, access to health care, cloning, and euthanasia. The states are key battlegrounds for public policy on all of these issues and more. Religious groups that seek influence on them must be involved at this level.

STATE CONFERENCES OF CATHOLIC BISHOPS NATIONALLY

The intersection of these two trends—the movement of the Catholic Church to the mainstream of American social and political life and the devolution of responsibility for some key aspects of public policy from the federal government to the states—suggests the importance of a state-level study of the political advocacy of conferences of Catholic bishops across the United States. Already in 1992, political scientists Timothy Byrnes and Mary Segers had noted, "churches represent God, if you will, not only in Washington but in Hartford, Trenton, Baton Rouge, Tallahassee, Albany, Springfield, and Harrisburg as well. Put simply, state-level issues and state-level politics require state-level lobbying on the part of religious spokesmen." In this respect, "few American institutions can match the Catholic Church in organizational strength at the *state* level."[23] Currently, the church is represented by a conference of Catholic bishops in 33 of the 50 states and the District of Columbia.

The majority of state Catholic conferences were established not in response to the new federalism, but as a result of the Second Vatican Council (1963–1965). Twenty-two of the thirty-four currently existing state Catholic conferences were founded prior to 1970, and the oldest conferences even predate Vatican II. The New York State Catholic Committee was established in 1916, the Illinois Catholic Committee for Legislation was founded in the early 1940s, and a Catholic lobby group in New Jersey was organized in 1947. In two other states the bishops were formally organized as a "conference" before the Council: the Catholic Conference of Ohio (established in 1945) and the Pennsylvania Catholic Conference (established in 1960). Despite these pre-conciliar precedents, the formalization and growth of state Catholic conferences was clearly inspired by Vatican II. Eighteen state conferences (53 percent of the current total) were founded in the four-year window from 1966 to 1970. (See table A.1 in appendix A for a list of all currently existing conferences and their year of founding.)

Thus, in comparison to other religious advocacy organizations, state Catholic conferences were better situated to meet the devolution of responsibility for public policy to the states. For example, in an essay published in 1992, Spencer McCoy Clapp mentioned the emerging "God Squad"—full-time religious lobbyists—in the Connecticut legislature. But William Wholean, the chief lobbyist for the church and the executive director of the Connecticut Catholic Conference at the time, had been in his position for nearly a quarter century (since the conference's founding in 1969), earning him the title "dean of the God Squad."[24]

Despite their long history, state Catholic conferences are frequently overlooked even by astute students of the role of Catholicism in politics. In the conclusion of his 1991 book *Catholic Bishops in American Politics*, which focuses predominantly on the activities of the United States Catholic Conference, Timothy Byrnes speculated that there may be a return to the local emphasis that characterized the bishops' involvement in political life in the eighteenth and nineteenth centuries. He rightly pointed to the 1989 *Webster* decision and the "neofederalism" that was ascendant at the time. But he failed to note a critical difference between the late nineteenth and the late twentieth centuries: The contemporary political movement would not only be back to local dioceses but to state-level episcopal conferences as well. Similarly, in discussing the aftermath of *Roe v. Wade*, both sociologist Gene Burns and theologian Chester Gillis gloss over the state level. Burns reports that "the bishops' outrage at the Court decision led to the American Church's most sustained, uncompromising effort (at the national, diocesan, and parish levels) ever to change particular U.S. laws." Gillis observes that "the bishops would fight this ruling nationally through the NCCB, in the states by the dioceses, and locally through the parishes." Both neglect the fact that state Catholic conferences have been key vehicles for engaging the abortion question in the states, both before and after *Roe*. A notable recent exception is the work of historian John McGreevy, which highlights the central role played by the Michigan Catholic Conference's "aggressive outreach campaign" in the defeat of a 1972 referendum in Michigan that would have allowed abortions for any reason through the twentieth week of pregnancy.[25]

But the omission of state Catholic conferences from the story of American Catholicism is not surprising. Although state Catholic conferences are the functional equivalents of the United States Conference of Catholic Bishops, no one has ever published a systematic social scientific study of their work.[26] Byrnes and Segers recognized this oversight in their volume on *The Catholic Church and the Politics of Abortion: A View from the States.* "We have come away from our work on this book," they write, "convinced that students of American Catholicism have to this point paid insufficient attention to the various state Catholic conferences around the country. These conferences represent the bishops of a given state in the political arena, and they vary substantially in terms of their cohesiveness and institutional viability. On the whole, these conferences are a crucial element in the Catholic Church's participation in the American political process. . . . State conferences, and the very significant differences among them, offer fertile ground for further study and analysis."[27] This statement is as true today as it was in 1992 when their book was published.

Byrnes and Segers, I am sure, would join me in wholeheartedly agreeing with Woodstock Center fellow William Bole's characterization of these organizations as "one of the church's better-kept secrets."[28] This book seeks to divulge that secret, for the benefit of students of American religion and politics, as well as for all those concerned with the public role of religion in American democratic life and institutions as we progress in the new millennium.

NOTES

1. For a more comprehensive treatment of welfare reform in Wisconsin, see Thomas J. Corbett, "Welfare Reform in Wisconsin: The Rhetoric and the Reality," pp. 19–54 in Donald Norris and Lyke Thompson, eds., *The Politics of Welfare Reform* (Thousand Oaks, CA: Sage Publications, 1995).

2. Clark G. Radatz, "Wisconsin Works (W-2): A Brief Description," Brief 96-1, *Wisconsin Briefs from the Legislative Reference Bureau*, June 1996.

3. Wisconsin Catholic Conference, *Capital Report*, October 1995.

4. Rembert Weakland, "Wisconsin Works: Breaking a Covenant," *Washington Post*, 4 July 1996, p. A29.

5. Douglas Schewe, *Capital Times*, 10 July 1996; "Church, State Clash Over Roles," *Wisconsin State Journal*, 10 July 1996.

6. "Governor Shouldn't 'Stick It' to Archbishop," *The Sheboygan Press*, 10 July 1996; Mike Flaherty, "Thompson Lashes Out at Archbishop," *Wisconsin State Journal*, 9 July 1996; "King Tommy and the Turbulent Priest," *Capital Times*, 14 July 1996.

7. "Holy Terror," *Capital Times*, 10 July 1996.

8. Mark Chaves, *Secularization in the Twentieth Century United States* (unpublished doctoral dissertation, Harvard University, 1991), pp. 292–93.

9. According to Tschannen, although the secularization paradigm "is not completely represented in any one of the theories" of its various carriers, "its core element—*differentiation*—is shared by them all" (Olivier Tschannen, "The Secularization Paradigm: A Systematization," *Journal for the Scientific Study of Religion* 30 [1991]: 395–415, quote on p. 403). This is most evident in *Public Religions in the Modern World* (Chicago: University of Chicago Press, 1994), an award-winning book in which Jose Casanova has gone so far as to say "the theory of secularization is nothing more than a subtheory of general theories of differentiation" (p. 18). This is taking the point a bit too far since it excludes secularization at the individual and organizational levels, but it does correctly assert the predominance of societal-level institutional differentiation in theories of secularization. See also Mark Chaves, "Secularization as Declining Religious Authority," *Social Forces* 72 (1994): 749–74; Philip Gorski, "Historicizing the Secularization Debate: Church, State, and Society in Late Medieval and Early Modern Europe (ca. 1300 to 1700)," *American Sociological Review* 65, no. 1 (February 2000): 138–68.

In recent years, several sociologists have launched a wholesale assault on the reality of secularization (see especially Rodney Stark, "Secularization, R.I.P.," *Sociology of Religion* 60, no. 3 [1999]: 249–274; R. Stephen Warner, "Work in Progress Toward a New Paradigm for the Sociological Study of Religion in the United States," *American Journal of Sociology* 98 [1993]: 1044–93). Even Peter Berger, who had previously gone to the mat for secularization in his conference bout with Andrew Greeley, has famously disclaimed secularization theory in an interview with *The Christian Century* (29 October 1997): "I think what I and most other sociologists of religion wrote in the 1960s about secularization was a mistake. Our underlying argument was that secularization and modernity go hand in hand. With more modernization comes more secularization. It wasn't a crazy theory. There was some evidence for it. But I think it's basically wrong." But this same Peter Berger has also famously commented that if Indians are the most religious people in the world and Swedes are the least religious, then Americans are a nation of Indians ruled by an elite of Swedes. That a scholar as learned as Berger could at one moment dispute the reality of secularization and at another moment point to its obvious manifestation is one of the frustrations of even mentioning the term.

10. Roy Wallis and Steve Bruce, "Secularization: Trends, Data, and Theory," *Research in the Social Scientific Study of Religion* 3 (1991): 4; Casanova, *Public Religions*, pp. 19, 37; Donald Smith, *Religion and Political Development* (Boston: Little, Brown, 1970), p. 2, quoted in Richard Gelm, *Politics and Religious Authority: American Catholics Since the Second Vatican Council* (Westport, CA: Greenwood Press, 1994), p. 13.

11. Wolfgang Schluchter, *Rationalism, Religion, and Domination: A Weberian Perspective* (Berkeley: University of California Press, 1989), pp. 261, 263.

12. Casanova, *Public Religions*, pp. 39, 43.

13. A term I stole from Karl Polanyi, who used it in a different context and sense in *The Great Transformation* (Boston: Beacon, 1944).

14. Crane Brinton, "Enlightenment," in *The Encyclopedia of Philosophy*, vol. 2 (New York: Macmillan Publishing and Free Press, 1967), p. 520.

15. John McGreevy, "Thinking on One's Own: Catholicism in the American Intellectual Imagination, 1928–1960," *Journal of American History* 84 (June 1997): 98, 99, 125.

16. Andrew Greeley, "After Secularity: The Neo-Gemeinschaft Society: A Post-Christian Postscript," *Sociological Analysis* 27 (Fall 1966): 119–20; George Weigel, "Taking America Seriously: Catholicism and the American Future," pp. 1–22 in Richard John Neuhaus and George Weigel, eds., *Being Christian Today: An American Conversation* (Washington, DC: Ethics and Public Policy Center, 1992), p. 16.

17. Richard John Neuhaus, *The Catholic Moment: The Paradox of the Church in the Postmodern World* (San Francisco: Harper & Row, 1987), p. 283. See also Neuhaus, *The Naked Public Square: Religion and Democracy in America*, 2nd ed. (Grand Rapids, MI: Eerdmans, 1986), p. 262.

18. Casanova, *Public Religions*, chapter 7 on the United States and chapter 4 on Poland.

19. Richard Gelm, *Politics and Religious Authority: American Catholics Since the Second Vatican Council* (Westport, CT: Greenwood Press, 1994), p. 90.

20. Carl Van Horn, "The Quiet Revolution," in Carl Van Horn, ed., *The State of the States* (Washington, DC: Congressional Quarterly Press, 1989), p. 1.

21. David Hedge, *Governance and the Changing American States* (Boulder, CO: Westview Press, 1998), p. xi.

22. Michael Berkman and Robert O'Connor, "Do Women Legislators Matter? Female Legislators and State Abortion Policy," *American Politics Quarterly* 21 (1993): 112.

23. Timothy Byrnes and Mary Segers, "Introduction," pp. 1–13 in Timothy Byrnes and Mary Segers, eds., *The Catholic Church and the Politics of Abortion: A View from the States* (Boulder, CO: Westview Press, 1992), pp. 10, 2.

24. Spencer McCoy Clapp, "Leading the Nation After *Webster*: Connecticut's Abortion Law," pp. 118–36 in Byrnes and Segers, eds., *The Catholic Church and the Politics of Abortion*, pp. 124–25.

25. Timothy Byrnes, *Catholic Bishops in American Politics* (Princeton, NJ: Princeton University Press, 1991); Gene Burns, *The Frontiers of Catholicism: The Politics of Ideology in a Liberal World* (Berkeley: University of California Press, 1992), p. 106; Chester Gillis, *Roman Catholicism in America* (New York: Columbia University Press, 1999), p. 183; John McGreevy, *Catholicism and American Freedom: A History* (New York: W.W. Norton, 2003), p. 277.

26. As will be discussed at greater length in chapter 2, one dissertation in canon law has been written on state Catholic conferences, and a summary article based on that work was published in a journal of The Catholic University of America's School of Canon Law. See Michael Sheehan, "State Catholic Conferences," *The Jurist* 35 (1975): 431–54.

27. Byrnes and Segers, "Introduction," p. 10.

28. William Bole, "What Do State Catholic Conferences Do?" pp. 92–109 in Margaret O'Brien Steinfels, ed., *American Catholics and Civic Engagement: A Distinctive Voice* (Lanham, MD: Rowman & Littlefield, 2004), p. 94.

1

History

From John Carroll to the Maryland Catholic Conference

The Catholic Church from its inception has been involved in public life. The involvement of Catholic bishops in American politics, therefore, is not novel. But the scale, scope, and style of the bishops' engagement has clearly changed over time. In particular, their organization into state Catholic conferences is an innovation worthy of attention. This chapter provides some of the backstory for understanding the role of the Catholic Church in state politics today, beginning with the establishment of Maryland as a Catholic colony and the appointment of John Carroll of Baltimore as the first American bishop. It concludes with a comprehensive description of one contemporary bishops' conference, the Maryland Catholic Conference.

The development of the Catholic Church in America has in many ways paralleled the development of the United States as a nation. Some of the most interesting and important developments center on "the old line state," Maryland.[1] *Terra Maria* was named by King Charles after his wife, Queen Henrietta Maria, when he gave the charter for the colony to the Calvert family in 1632. The Calverts were a Catholic family, and Maryland was therefore seen as a safe haven for Catholics fleeing religious persecution in England. But the Calverts also sought to ensure that religious freedom for all Christians would apply in Maryland. Colonial officials were to take the following oath: "I will make no difference of persons in conferring offices, favors and rewards for or in respect of religion, but merely as they shall be found faithful and well deserving and imbued with moral virtues and abilities."[2] Although this was particularly important for Catholics in England, it also appealed to many Protestants who would live in a colony owned by a Catholic family. In the end, a majority of those the Calverts signed up to colonize Maryland were Protestants.

Some 140 colonists, including two Jesuit priests, departed from England in November 1633 on the 350-ton *Ark*, accompanied by the 50-ton *Dove*. They sailed under the leadership of Cecil Calvert's brother, Leonard, who would act as governor of the colony while Lord Baltimore remained in England to defend his family's colonial rights. They arrived in America the following spring. On March 25, 1634, the company disembarked on St. Clement's Island in the Potomac River. One of the Jesuit priests in the traveling party, Andrew White, described the scene as follows:

> On the day of the Annunciation of the Most Holy Virgin Mary we celebrated mass for the first time in this island: this had never been done before in this region of the world. When mass was over, we took an enormous cross, which we had hewn out of a tree, on our shoulders, proceeded in rank to a designated place and, with the help of the governor, his associates, and the remaining Catholics, erected a monument to Christ, our Savior, while we humbly recited the Litany of the Cross on bended knee, with much emotion.[3]

Shortly thereafter, the colonists settled in what is now the southern tip of Maryland, naming their first village and the capital of the Maryland Colony *St. Mary's City* in honor of the Queen and the Blessed Virgin.

According to its charter, colonial Maryland was to have its own government with limited power. In February 1635, the first General Assembly met at St. Mary's City, which served as the capital of Maryland for 60 years. After King William and Queen Mary revoked the Calvert family's charter and made Maryland a royal colony, the capital was relocated further up Chesapeake Bay. In 1694, Maryland's royal governor Francis Nicholson decided to relocate the capital to Anne Arundel Town and rename it Annapolis in honor of Princess Anne. Only Santa Fe, Boston, and Providence have served as state capitals longer than Annapolis.

The Maryland statehouse is the oldest in continuous use in the United States, noted for both its wooden dome (constructed without nails so as to avoid British taxes) and its lightning rod (constructed in accordance with Benjamin Franklin's recommendations, the largest such rod ever attached to a building in Franklin's lifetime). The building would house the nation's government from November 1783 to

June 1784 under the Articles of Confederation. It was there, during this time, where George Washington famously resigned his commission as commander in chief of the Continental Army (on December 23, 1783) and the Congress of the Confederation ratified the Treaty of Paris, which ended the Revolutionary War (on February 14, 1784).

As Washington was entering the political scene and the dawn of a new nation was breaking, so too was the Catholic Carroll family and the Catholic Church in America. In November 1789—seven months after Washington was sworn in as the first president of the United States—Baltimore was established as the see city of the first American diocese, and John Carroll was elected its first bishop. In the words of historian Henry Browne, "As the new Republic was unified around the figure of George Washington, so the new American church was drawn together around John Carroll, its first bishop."[4]

Bishop Carroll was responsible for the entire church in America: one diocese, approximately 35 priests, six schools, and some 35,000 Catholics (0.8 percent of the U.S. population). According to historian Patrick Carey, as bishop, Carroll "took some major steps to form a national church . . . that would be adapted to the exigencies of the rising new nation."[5] A major part of his responsibility was defending the church as an institution and the compatibility of Roman Catholicism with the new nation's identity in the face of sometimes virulent anti-Catholicism. In other words, he had an important political role to play. This role was facilitated by his prominent family, particularly his cousin, Charles Carroll of Carrollton. Historian Thomas O'Brien Hanley notes of the political and religious freedom which was won in the late eighteenth century, "In the drama of revolution that unfolded, Maryland played her part, and the Carrolls were her most convincing protagonists. Charles Carroll's cousin helped formulate the Maryland bill for religious freedom, he himself signed the Declaration of Independence [the only Catholic to do so], and another cousin, Daniel, helped draft the First Amendment and signed the Constitution."[6]

Charles Carroll was president of the Maryland State Senate when Bishop Carroll wrote to him from Whitemarsh on November 11, 1783, about a state law that forbade Roman Catholics to be guardians of Protestant children:

> I have been informed that some time after the establishment of our present Constitution, a law was continued relating to the administration of Orphans estates, in which amongst other provisions was a clause

preventing Roman Catholicks from being guardians to Protestant children; & in consequence of this judgment a clause was obtained in the late Genl Court disabling one Philip Casey of Montgomery County from acting in that quality to his son in law. As this cause is inconsistent with that perfect equality of rights, which by our Constitution is secured to all Religions, I make no doubt but you will be able to obtain a general repeal of this and all other laws and clauses of laws enacting any partial regards to one denomination to the prejudice of others.[7]

Although being able to write his cousin makes this case somewhat unique, certain aspects of this intervention were typical of the church's involvement in politics in the early years of the Republic: it was undertaken by the bishop himself, and it was directed at the government within his own state. John England of Charleston, South Carolina, (1820–1842) was another early exemplar of this type of political involvement, as was John Hughes of New York (1842–1864). Indeed, "within New York City, the archbishop's residence has long been called 'the Powerhouse,'" in recognition of its role in government.[8]

This style of local advocacy made sense because, well into the nineteenth century, the governance of both the church and the new nation was highly decentralized. On the church side of the equation, each bishop has responsibility for his own diocese under canon law, answering only to Rome. On the state side, we find an extremely weak central political authority.[9] All things considered, Roman Catholicism is best characterized at the time as a "diocesan rights church in a states' rights political system."[10] The most important politics, especially those of interest to the church, were local and acted on locally. As political scientist Timothy Byrnes summarizes the situation of the young church and nation, "most of the hierarchy's salient political activities during the traditional era involved the relationships between individual bishops and local politicians and officials."[11] It was not until the highly centralized national governments emerged in the nineteenth century that bishops started to formally organize themselves into standing episcopal conferences.

THE RISE OF EPISCOPAL CONFERENCES

Episcopal conferences are an instance of what the church calls "episcopal collegiality." As such, they are not new. Councils, synods, and other gatherings have a long history in the church, including well-known and consequential early gatherings like the Council of Nicaea in 325. As Pope John Paul II has written, "Without prejudice to the power which each bishop enjoys by divine institution in his own particular Church, the consciousness of being part of an undivided body has caused bishops throughout the Church's history to employ, in fulfillment of their mission, means, structures and ways of communicating which express their communion and solicitude for all the Churches, and prolong the very life of the college of the apostles: pastoral cooperation, consultation, mutual assistance, etc."[12] What is novel about episcopal conferences as specific instances of episcopal collegiality is their "stable and permanent character."[13] Councils, synods, and other gatherings of bishops are episodic, but conferences operate continuously.

The history of episcopal conferences is generally considered to have begun in the first half of the nineteenth century with the rise of the modern nation-state and the separation of church and state. These developments required bishops to come together to engage new, centralized, secular governments. Among the earliest instances was when the bishops of Belgium met to discuss responses to the 1830 revolution there.[14] In 1889, the Vatican's Sacred Congregation of Bishops and Regulars first expressly called them by the name "episcopal conferences."[15] Popes Pius IX (1846–1878) and Leo XIII (1878–1903) encouraged these meetings of bishops, and conferences continued to grow into the twentieth century. "The 1959 *Annuario Pontificio* lists for the first time the forty-two conferences existing on the eve of the Second Vatican Council."[16]

Although the bishops of the United States did not establish an episcopal conference until the twentieth century, they regularly expressed their collegiality in the nineteenth century in various important councils and other regular meetings of leading prelates. When the Diocese of Baltimore *was* the hierarchy, there was no need for episcopal collegiality. But as the church grew and subdivided, efforts were made frequently to bring the church hierarchy together. According to American Catholic historian James Hennesey, S.J., "In the single century from 1783–1884 the entire American Church met in three general chapters of the clergy, a synod, a bishops' meeting, seven provincial councils that were also national councils, and three plenary councils. From 1890 on, the archbishops of the country, and later all the bishops, have met annually. No other nation, as far as I know, has such a record." Jay Dolan reports that the 35 major councils held in the United States from 1829 to 1900 "represented almost one-quarter of all the major councils held throughout the Catholic world during this period. The extent of this conciliar activity in the United States was even more striking when compared with the church in Europe that had 10 times as many dioceses but only forty-nine such councils from 1829 to 1900." Even after the passing of John Carroll, Baltimore continued to play a central role, hosting seven provincial and three plenary councils during the nineteenth century. It was at the Third Plenary Council in 1884—what church historian Gerald Fogarty, S.J., calls "Baltimore III"—that the bishops famously founded the Catholic University of America and issued the *Baltimore Catechism*. Baltimore III marked the end of bishops' councils in the United States, though the American archbishops (as the Board of Trustees of Catholic University) continued to meet annually from 1890 on "to confer on internal matters."[17]

The earliest *formal* organization of the Catholic bishops in America came in response to the entry of the United States into World War I in 1917. The impetus did not come from the bishops themselves, but from the editor of the Paulist publication *Catholic World*, Fr. John J. Burke, C.S.P. Burke wanted to create a national identity and organizational center for the church in response to the expansion of the state and the nationalization of politics during the late nineteenth and early twentieth centuries. Throughout its history, America has witnessed religiously inspired or religiously based social movements of all sorts, including the abolition and temperance movements. But as the state grew and became more formally organized, so too did religious politics.[18] The war effort gave Burke an opportunity to advocate for such an organization to represent the Catholic Church. Thus, the development of the National Catholic War Council (NCWC) under Burke's leadership was, according to Michael Zöller, representative of the nationalization, centralization, and professionalization of the church, in parallel fashion to that of the state.[19]

Burke first presented his idea to three American cardinals: James Gibbons of Baltimore, William Henry O'Connell of Boston, and John Farley of New York. As historian Elizabeth McKeown recounts, "After these prelates approved his plans, Burke wrote all dioceses and national Catholic societies, asking them to send representatives to a meeting at Catholic University of America in August 1917. There, he urged the 115 delegates to form the National Catholic War Council."[20] Although there were no bishops present at the meeting and the council would have a professional staff, "Burke insisted on placing the new organization under the direction of the archbishops." When the Board of Trustees of the Catholic University of America met in November 1917, they approved the plan.[21]

After the end of the war, Burke moved to continue the national organization by writing a "Memorandum on the Necessity of a Permanent National Committee with Headquarters at Washington for the Study, Advancement, Protection, and Promotion of Catholic Needs and Interests" (July 1919). According to McKeown, "Unless there was a representative organization in the capitol, Burke felt that Catholics would be unable to influence public opinion in the legislative process in directions favorable to Catholic interests. His experience with lobbyists, particularly those of the Federal Council of Churches and the Anti-Saloon League, convinced him that special interests could only be protected by organized effort." Meeting at Catholic University in September 1919, the bishops approved Burke's plan and named him to be general secretary of the organization. Burke and his staff would make the transition from National Catholic War Council to National Catholic Welfare Council.[22]

Not all American bishops were as supportive of the organization as, for example, Cardinal Gibbons of Baltimore. Fearing usurpation of their canonical authority over their dioceses, some opposed a national episcopal organization.[23] At the time the NCWC was established, episcopal conferences were not addressed in the 1917 *Codex Juris Canonici* (Code of Canon Law) and so had no legal status in the church. Cardinal O'Connell of Boston led the opposition to the NCWC and was supported by Bishops Charles McDonnell of Brooklyn and Archbishop Sebastian Messmer of Milwaukee. The opponents succeeded in getting the Consistorial Congregation of the Holy See to issue a letter in February 1922 ordering the suppression of the NCWC. A defense of the NCWC was mounted, with Bishop Joseph Schrembs of Cleveland and Archbishop Henry Moeller of Cincinnati traveling to Rome to represent the NCWC. In the end, Pope Pius XI revoked the decree of suppression, although the Vatican requested (among other things) that the NCWC change its title from "Council" to "Conference," so there would be no confusion of the national organization with a worldwide council.[24]

Over the next four decades, the NCWC represented the church in Washington, issuing statements and lobbying on matters of concern to the church in the world, very much in the tradition of the "Right Reverend New Dealer" Msgr. John Ryan (head of the NCWC Department of Social Action, 1919–1945) and his 1919 "Program of Social Reconstruction." The Conference largely stayed away from internal church matters during this time, which were seen as the province of each ordinary in his own see. According to Bishop William McManus, who served on the staff from 1945 to 1957, "The only purpose of the NCWC was to express the church's concern about the temporal affairs of the United States."[25] The collected pastoral letters of the American hierarchy, running now to six volumes covering 1792 to 1997, include 70 statements totaling almost 400 pages from the period 1919 to 1961. Among the issues treated during this time are the following: unemployment (1930), indecent literature (1932), peace and war (1939), federal aid to education (1944), secularism (1947), the child (1950), traffic safety (1957), and bigotry (1960).[26] Also, federal aid for Catholic schools was always central to the NCWC's lobbying efforts in Washington. Over time, though long after his death, Fr. Burke's original vision for the bishops' conference was realized: "the leadership of the conference did become Washington insiders. The NCWC did come to be perceived by politicians and other national interest groups as the 'voice' of American Catholicism, as it continued to act as the liaison between the church and the White House and Capitol Hill."[27]

Although it was well established by January 1959 when Pope John XXIII announced a worldwide (ecumenical) council for the purpose of *aggiornamento*, the NCWC would nonetheless be profoundly affected as the Second Vatican Council revolutionized the Catholic Church internally as well as in its relationship with the external world. According to Mary Hanna, Vatican II "reformed liturgy and ritual, but it also moved the church into far greater participation in social and political affairs. The council stressed that the church as an institution and Catholics in general had a positive obligation to involve themselves in the problems of the world; it issued a series of documents that denounced various political, social, and economic ills—poverty, illiteracy, political repression—as morally wrong under Christian doctrine; and it urged Catholics to work to alleviate them."[28] As historian John McGreevy argues, "American Catholics before the 1960s did not have a *theory* of civil engagement, only a haphazard set of encounters with non-Catholics in the public realm, often in direct defense of church interests."[29] The Second Vatican Council, therefore, "provided a theological rationale for a public Catholicism that had been the goal of numerous American Catholics since the early twentieth century."[30]

According to sociologist Jose Casanova, the "Pastoral Constitution on the Church in the Modern World [*Gaudium et Spes*] represents the lifting of the Catholic *anathema* that was hanging over modernity and the final acceptance of the legitimacy of the modern *saeculum*, of the modern age and of the modern world." Related to this acceptance of modernity is the Vatican II "Declaration on Religious Freedom" (*Dignitatis Humanae*). In this document, the Catholic Church for the first time recognizes the fundamental human right to freedom of conscience. In doing so, it also accepts the core of what is often called "The Murray Project" (after the influential Jesuit theologian John Courtney Murray): the disestablishment of religion and the separation of church and state. As a result, Catholicism would no longer seek the favor of the state as an established religion, nor would it seek to influence politics through church-sponsored political parties (recognizing that this was the European model, not the American one, which had always resembled in practice what Murray advocated in theory). Its public role, hereafter, would be as a voluntary association in civil society seeking to bring its moral perspective to bear on political issues, influencing but not dictating policy outcomes.[31]

Although not as well-known as *Gaudium et Spes* or *Dignitatis Humanae*, the Second Vatican Council's "Decree on the Bishops' Pastoral Office in the Church" (*Christus Dominus*) would prove most consequential for episcopal collegiality in general and national episcopal conferences like the NCWC in particular. The document "stresses the collective, collegial nature of the episcopate as successors to the college of the Apostles, who in communion with the Pope exercise jointly the pastoral and magisterial office of the entire church. The decree also . . . mandates the establishment of national and regional episcopal conferences."[32] *Christus Dominus* defines a conference as "a form of assembly in which the bishops of a given country or region exercise their pastoral office jointly in order to enhance the Church's beneficial influence on all men, especially by devising forms of the apostolate and apostolic methods suitably adapted to the circumstances of the times" (no. 38:1). This decree was reinforced by Pope Paul VI's subsequent call for episcopal conferences to be established wherever they did not yet exist.[33] *Christus Dominus* concludes by prescribing "that in the revision of the code of canon law suitable laws be drawn up in keeping with the principles stated in this decree" (no. 44). The 1983 revision of the *Codex* does include specific treatment of episcopal conferences (see canons 447–59). The definition of conferences of bishops in Canon 447 repeats that given in *Christus Dominus* (no. 38:1).

These developments led the bishops of the United States, meeting at the Catholic University of America in November 1966, to create the National Conference of Catholic Bishops (NCCB) and to reorganize the NCWC as the United States Catholic Conference (USCC).[34] As Gerald Fogarty summarizes the distinction, the NCCB is "a canonical entity consisting of all the bishops of the nation to enable them to exchange views and jointly exercise their pastoral ministry." In contrast, the USCC is "a civil entity whereby the bishops join with others in fostering voluntary collective action on the interdiocesan level in areas such as educational and social concerns of the church."[35] Already in his 1992 analysis of the U.S. bishops conference, *A Flock of Shepherds*, Thomas Reese, S.J., noted that the distinction between the NCCB and USCC "proved difficult to maintain." In July 2001, the two structures were merged into a single United States Conference of Catholic Bishops (USCCB), though this "reorganization" has changed the day-to-day operations of the conference very little.

Michael Zöller observes that the "growth and significance" of the national bishops' organization "is already discernible in the fact that a remodeled school building that had served as the NCWC's headquarters since 1919 was replaced first by a much larger building and then in 1989 by a separate office complex."[36] The new complex in Northwest Washington, D.C., down the street from the Basilica of the Shrine of the Immaculate Conception and Catholic University, is known by some of the staff as "The Big House" because its four stories house 400-plus employees of the USCCB.

With its large and growing staff and budget, the U.S. bishops conference has been extremely productive over the past three-plus decades, continuing to issue statements and lobby on an ever-widening range of issues, as well as addressing internal church matters of all sorts. In the public policy arena, in addition to staples such as social welfare and education, the post-Vatican II bishops conference has dealt with the aftermath of the Supreme Court's decision in

Roe v. Wade, the legalization of capital punishment, the escalation of the nuclear arms race, and a host of emerging issues such as farmers and farm workers, environmental concerns, euthanasia, the legalization of same sex marriage, and all manner of biotechnology issues including cloning. Thus, the bishops' political involvement took seriously the ethos of *Gaudium et Spes* and moved from being primarily defensive of Catholic "institutional interests" to a more affirmative engagement with the world, including a greater willingness to assume a critical posture toward the government.

Nowhere was this clearer than in the bishops' statements on peace, *The Challenge of Peace: God's Promise and Our Response* (1983), and the economy, *Economic Justice for All* (1986). As with Ryan's "Program of Social Reconstruction" decades earlier, these documents were not well received by some conservative Catholics who believed the bishops went beyond their competence as religious leaders in making specific diagnoses of social problems and prescribing specific policy remedies. But they did have an effect on the debates over war and peace and economic justice, and elevated the bishops' standing in the public arena at the same time. To wit, John Carr, the current director of the USCCB's Department of Social Development and World Peace, recalls a meeting of his staff with General Colin Powell, who was then chairman of the Joint Chiefs of Staff. Powell arrived at the meeting with a dog-eared and highlighted copy of *The Challenge of Peace* and declared, "I think sometimes we take this more seriously than you do."

ENTER THE MARYLAND CATHOLIC CONFERENCE

As we enter the third millennium, the hierarchy of the Catholic Church continues to engage the public life of the nation, in defense of both church interests and the common good. But the conditions and manner of this engagement have changed dramatically over the two centuries since John Carroll was the entire American church hierarchy. Carroll's successor, the fourteenth archbishop of Baltimore, is William Cardinal Keeler. Keeler is responsible for 500,178 Catholics and 154 parishes in the Baltimore Archdiocese, which is now just one of 175 Latin Rite Catholic dioceses in the United States and one of three dioceses that cover part of the state of Maryland. From Carroll's time to Keeler's, the church and nation have grown, politics and policy have become more complex, and the church's agenda has become broader and more proactive. Consequently, the archbishop's political involvement has become collectivized and professionalized.

Keeler's political activity in Maryland today is undertaken in communion with Archbishop Theodore McCarrick of Washington, D.C. (whose archdiocese includes five Maryland counties), and Bishop Michael Saltarelli of Wilmington, Delaware (whose diocese includes the Eastern Shore of Maryland). Together, these bishops form the core of the Board of Governors of the Maryland Catholic Conference, with Keeler serving as the chairman.[37] When the bishops engage in political advocacy, they do so principally through the lay professionals who staff the Conference. Like many state Catholic conferences, the Maryland Catholic Conference was founded in 1967, immediately following the Second Vatican Council. According to their 2003 Legislative Handbook, "The Conference is our institutional ambassador to the public square. There, armed with Gospel values and Church teaching, it advocates for the just and compassionate resolution of public-policy issues that affect all of us and virtually all aspects of family and community life, issues involving human rights, social justice, and the life of the Church in society."

In addition to Keeler, McCarrick, and Saltarelli, all of the auxiliary bishops of Baltimore and Washington (currently six) serve on the Maryland Catholic Conference's Board of Governors. The board meets twice per year and has the power to approve policies and priorities of the Conference. Issues that reach the board of governors have typically been developed by the Conference staff in consultation with the Conference's administrative board and departments. The 17-member administrative board, composed largely of laypeople experienced in public policy, meets two times per year, immediately prior to the board of governors meetings. Each of the three dioceses serving Maryland appoints five members to the administrative board, and one seat each is occupied by the state deputy of the Maryland Knights of Columbus Council and an executive of a Catholic hospital in Maryland. The most recent addition to this board is the appropriately named John Carroll Byrnes, a recently retired Baltimore City Circuit Court judge and former member of the Maryland State Senate.[38]

The administrative board concept was introduced soon after Keeler's arrival, when the Conference's bylaws were revised to reflect a new organizational structure. As envisioned by Richard J. "Dick" Dowling, the executive director, the board would consist of lay Catholics who understood church teaching and its relevance to matters being debated in the public forum. Such individuals also would have experience in public affairs, familiarity with policy processes, and easy access to movers and shakers in government, the political and business communities, and the media—individuals who could make the kinds of connections the Conference would need to advance its advocacy mission. But when the three Maryland diocesan bishops made their initial appointments, they turned to trusted clergy lieutenants, men who worked for them in their diocesan offices. "The early meetings were deadly," Dowling says now. "Virtually none of the first appointees were familiar with public policy or the processes of government and some, I think, were fearful that anything they said say might somehow offend their patrons. The guidance we were looking for just wasn't forthcoming." In time, that would change. In addition to Judge Byrnes and the Knights of Columbus and hospitals' representatives, the current administrative board includes a former leadership member of the state legislature, a former governor's chief counsel, the one-time president of the Raskob Foundation for Catholic Activities, the social-programs director of the state's most populous county, and the president of the largest car dealership on Maryland's Eastern Shore, himself a former county councilman.

The administrative board, in turn, is advised by three "departments," each of which has a distinct focus. The Social Concerns Department focuses on poverty and health care; the Justice, Pro-Life, and Human Rights Department on abortion, capital punishment, civil rights, family, and pornography; and the Education Department on elementary and secondary education, particularly but not exclusively related to nonpublic schools. Each department is effectively a committee composed of three representatives from each of the three Maryland dioceses, both church employees and parishioners who work in the departments' areas of concern. The departments meet at least four times per year and make recommendations to the administrative board. Each department is counseled by a member of the Maryland Catholic Conference staff and has a member designated as the "moderator" who carries forward its recommendations.[39]

The Conference's "secretariat" currently consists of an executive director, three associate directors, a communications associate, an office manager, and a part-time bookkeeper. These six and a half full-time staff are considerably more than the two full-time staff employed by the Conference for much of its early history. Two important turning points in the Conference's history were the hiring of Dowling as executive director in 1984 and the appointment of Keeler to the Primatial See of Baltimore. A veteran of Washington, D.C., politics, Dowling served as legislative and press assistant to U.S. congressman and senator William D. Hathaway (D-Maine) from 1968 to 1972, director of government relations for the American Speech and Hearing Association from 1972 to 1979, and executive director of the American Society of Allied Health Professions from 1979 to 1982. In the years just prior to his employment by the Maryland bishops, he was a national fellow of the W. K. Kellogg Foundation, the first person chosen for the prestigious program from outside academia. Over the past two decades, Dowling has gradually and significantly upgraded the Maryland Catholic Conference staff and operations.

This was aided by the installation, in 1989, of William Keeler as archbishop of Baltimore. Keeler came to Baltimore having served as bishop of Harrisburg, Pennsylvania, from 1983 to 1989. Part of his responsibilities as bishop of Harrisburg, the capital of Pennsylvania, was to serve as president of the Pennsylvania Catholic Conference. During his service in Harrisburg, Dowling suggests, Keeler "came to understand the need for Church involvement in the public square, to appreciate advocacy's role in advancing Church interests. What's more, he came to respect the role politicians play and, as a spectator, to enjoy the rough and tumble of their game." His interest in episcopal collegiality is reflected in his election as vice president of the National Conference of Catholic Bishops (NCCB) in 1989 and his subsequent election as NCCB president in 1992. He brings that enthusiasm to the Maryland Catholic Conference as well.

When Dowling took over the Maryland Catholic Conference from Francis X. McIntyre, who had served as the third executive director from 1978 to 1984, the functioning staff was himself and a secretary, and the scope of the Conference's operations was quite limited. "Before I was hired," Dowling recalls,

the Maryland Catholic Conference was regarded by the Baltimore Archdiocese as its pro-life advocate. The Archdiocese wanted to manage its own anti-poverty advocacy and had assigned two of its Catholic Charities employees to that work. Health-care issues, the death penalty, the environment, and various other concerns went virtually unattended. Meantime, the Archdiocese of Washington expected a full range of advocacy from the Conference, but since the Conference's bylaws put the chairmanship in the hands of the bishop of the primatial see, Baltimore had its way. In frustration, the Washington Archdiocese hired its own lobbyist. So when I arrived, three other church lobbyists were already on the scene, more often than not reading from different scripts.

In short order, at Dowling's behest, the Baltimore and Washington archbishops agreed that the church should have but one voice in the state capital, and the other operations were shut down.

At the beginning of Dowling's tenure, the Maryland Catholic Conference's headquarters were at St. Mary's Seminary in Baltimore. "The office was on the second floor, a beautiful office with a high ceiling, oak paneling, plush carpets, a great view of the campus, and about the last place a public policy outfit should be headquartered. It was in North Baltimore, a long way from Annapolis." After six months, Dowling moved the office to downtown Baltimore, across Cathedral Street from the archdiocesan offices. "For the time being, though, that's as far as I could get. I rented space in Annapolis during the 90-day legislation session, but moved back to Baltimore when the session ended. Cardinal Keeler's predecessor wanted it that way and, despite the contrary view held by his Washington counterpart, the Baltimore view in the matter prevailed." It took five more years and a new archbishop of Baltimore before Dowling succeeded in moving the Conference's office to the state capital.

The Maryland Catholic Conference now occupies half of a three-story house in Annapolis that has been converted into offices. From the third floor of the house on Duke of Gloucester Street, you can look across the rooftops on Main Street and State Circle and have a clear view of the famous statehouse dome. By cutting through two alleyways, the staff can walk to the statehouse and legislative offices in a few minutes. On the walk over, they might pass the opulent new office of the Maryland State Teachers Association (MSTA) on Main Street. As a 501(c)(3) organization, the Maryland Catholic Conference doesn't participate in the campaign financing and candidate endorsements the MSTA and other influential, big-money political organizations do. The Conference's modest rented space is symbolic of its

insider-outsider status. It is a respected lobbying organization in Annapolis *despite* not having the economic and political resources of
other major interest groups in the state.

In addition to moving its offices, Dowling has also incrementally
increased the size of the Conference staff. He hired his first associate in 1990. When he hired a second in 1991, he divided their
responsibilities—one associate responsible for "social concerns"
and the other for "justice, pro-life, and human rights." Currently, the
associate director for social concerns is Jeff Caruso, who earned his
J.D. from the University of Notre Dame Law School in 1996 and
joined the staff in 1998. The associate director for justice, pro-life,
and human rights is Dr. Nancy Fortier (a Ph.D. in analytical chem-
istry), whose volunteer activism in the pro-life movement gradually
overtook her professional work for Procter & Gamble, leading her
to join the Conference staff in 2002. A third associate was brought
on board in 1995 with primary responsibility for education. From
1995 to 2000, Mary Ellen Russell served as the associate for education. Russell then took a job in the United States Conference of
Catholic Bishops' Department of Education, where she worked from
2000 until 2002, at which time she returned to the Maryland Catholic
Conference. Dowling himself covers all areas of concern to the Conference and is especially involved in strategy, networking, and what
he calls "problematic issues" (which, as we will see, inevitably arise
in the legislatures). These four individuals are the core of the Maryland Catholic Conference's advocacy team. They are assisted by
communications associate Erin Appel, whose position was created
in 2001; office manager Christine Santo; and part-time bookkeeper
Patti Reigert. During legislative sessions, the staff grows by more
than half. In each of the past 10 years, it has been augmented by as
many as three part-time interns from Mount Saint Mary's College.
More recently, it has been joined by two volunteer advocates: H.
William Bauersfeld, a retired lobbyist for the state's Department of
General Services, and Patricia Kelly, who served for a decade as the
Maryland Catholic Conference's associate director for justice, pro-
life, and human rights prior to her "retirement."

The Maryland Catholic Conference's annual legislative agenda is developed by the staff and the departments, informed and refined by the
administrative board, and ultimately approved by the board of governors. In line with the tradition of Catholic Social Teaching—as em-

bodied in the documents of the Second Vatican Council and elaborated in the encyclical letters of Pope John Paul II—the foundation for all of the Conference's advocacy is the *dignity of the human person*. In their brochure "Building Blocks for Catholic Advocacy," the Maryland Catholic Conference declares, "We believe that all Marylanders— rich and poor, young and old, born and unborn, male and female, native-born and immigrant—possess a human dignity that is priceless and that must not be compromised."[40] This is reiterated in the theme of their 2003 lobby night (which brings lay Catholics to Annapolis to meet with legislators): "Human Dignity . . . Priceless!"

Concretely, this view is manifested in wide-ranging and diverse legislative priorities for the 2003 session. Among the 18 priorities listed in a brochure produced for the 2003 lobby night are the following:

- Support legislation to maintain annual funding at the current level for the Electric Universal Service Program.
- Support an increase in cash-assistance grants to eligible families with children.
- Support legislation to impose a two-year moratorium on executions.
- Support continued funding for the state's textbook-loan program for nonpublic school students.
- Support legislation that allows recipients of the Maryland Teacher Scholarship to perform their service requirement by teaching in a nonpublic school as well as a public school.
- Support legislation to remove the requirement that immigrants residing in Maryland pay out-of-state tuition at state universities.
- Support legislation to ensure that parents are involved in health-care decisions of their children, including a minor daughter's abortion/childbirth decisions.
- Redirect state Medicaid funding for abortion toward critical health-care needs.

Armed with this legislative agenda, the Conference staff immerse themselves in the political process for the 90 days the Maryland General Assembly meets each year.

I visited the Maryland Catholic Conference in the final week of the 417th legislative session (dating back to the first session held at St. Mary's City in 1635), which began on January 8, 2003. The legislature was scheduled to adjourn on April 7, but the budget had not yet been approved, and the question of legalizing slot machines to ease the state's $1.2 billion budget shortfall had yet to be resolved. The Conference staff also had a few issues of concern still alive. Jeff Caruso was working to maintain the level of cash assistance for the poor in the state budget and to kill a bill that would prohibit faith-based social service agencies (such as Catholic Charities) that sign procurement contracts with the state from discriminating against potential employees on the basis of sexual orientation. Nancy Fortier was preparing testimony against a bill that would require individuals to provide written advanced directives for embryos created during the in-vitro fertilization process. Mary Ellen Russell was monitoring the status of the Maryland Teacher Scholarship legislation and the inclusion of continued funding for a three-year-old textbook loan program in the annual budget. In addition to their individual responsibilities, especially at this time of year, all staff members have to be conversant with all the Conference's issues because a legislator may stop them at any time and ask, "Where is the Catholic Conference on this?"

In these waning days of the legislative session, Dick Dowling was mostly occupied with legislation that is nowhere in the Conference's legislative agenda. Inevitably, issues come up that are either unexpected or unwelcome (and often both), and the staff must be prepared to address them. In 2003, the unwelcome (though not unexpected) legislation was the result of the clergy sexual abuse scandal that rocked the Catholic Church in 2002. As in many other states, a bill was introduced in Maryland's session addressing the issue of clergy as mandatory reporters of child abuse. Current law requires all Maryland citizens to report suspected child abuse, though there is an exemption for clergy who learn of abuse from a person seeking their spiritual guidance (including, of course, in sacramental confession). The legislation introduced in 2003 would eliminate this exemption.

As Dowling was working behind the scenes to kill the bill, Cardinal McCarrick took up the issue in his weekly "Thinking of You" column in the archdiocese of Washington newspaper, the *Catholic Standard*. McCarrick wrote,

> What they are proposing is a grave violation of our Church's Canon Law, and I must oppose it with whatever authority I have, and you, dear friends, need to know this.

If this bill were to pass, I shall instruct all the priests in the Archdiocese of Washington who serve in Maryland to ignore it and to indicate they are acting on direct orders from me as their archbishop and religious superior. On this issue, I will gladly plead civil disobedience and willingly—if not gladly—go to jail. . . . I cannot allow three state senators and eight members of the House of Delegates who are the proposers of this legislation to force our priests to violate the sacramental seal of Confession. If there is a gauntlet involved in this process, then I throw it down now. While there is still time to prevent this attack on the sacramental seal of Confession, I ask you to write or phone your own state legislators in Annapolis and tell them how you feel about the proposed law and how it affects your rights as a Catholic American and a citizen of this state of Maryland. If in spite of all you do, it gets into law, I'm happy to assure you that, even behind bars, I'll be thinking of you.

Dowling's lobbying and the complaints generated by McCarrick's column resulted in the rejection of the Senate version of the bill by a unanimous Senate Judicial Proceedings Committee. An identical House version was withdrawn by its sponsor after three erstwhile co-sponsors, each of them a Catholic, asked to have their names removed from the measure.[41]

Two weeks later, the Senate Committee favorably reported out another bill introduced in reaction to the abuse scandal: a proposal to extend the statute of limitations for civil child sexual abuse actions. In its original form, the bill sought to extend the statute of limitations prospectively, from three to fifteen years, giving purported victims until their thirty-third birthdays to file claims for money damages. It also contained a retroactive aspect, permitting decades-old child-abuse claims against alleged perpetrators and their employers. A House version, generally similar in purpose to the Senate bill, sought to couple civil claims to criminal proceedings; a child-abuse action for money damages could be instituted at any time during the three-year period that begins with a final judgment in a criminal proceeding related to the same abuse allegation. Like the Senate bill, the measure featured a retroactive application. The Conference knew that while most Senate committee members wanted to avoid a retroactive application of the statute of limitations, they also wanted to avoid doing nothing. When Dowling offered amendments that stripped the measure's retroactivity and extended the statute of limitations for four years, or until a purported victim's twenty-fifth birthday, a committee majority went for them. The amended bill was approved six to five.

"I think it's a reasonable compromise," Dowling told the *Washington Post.* Several days later, the committee-approved version was passed by a unanimous Senate (46 to 0) and sent to the House of Delegates where, in the Judiciary Committee, it joined the bill tying civil child-abuse actions to criminal proceedings.[42]

Uncomfortable with the apples-and-oranges nature of the House-initiated bill, the House committee rejected the measure outright and began focusing its attention on the Senate-passed version. But some members of the panel were also dissatisfied with the Senate's product, and one of them, the committee's vice chairman, pressed his colleagues to support an amendment he was drafting to add twenty-one years to the Senate bill's four-year statute of limitations extension. On hearing of the new threat, Dowling exhorted staff members whose lobbying plates did not include other immediate-attention concerns to apply a "full-court press" against the amendment.

To this end, Jeff Caruso found two Judiciary Committee members in their offices about an hour prior to an 8:00 p.m., Monday evening floor session. Both were Democrats, one a moderate from a blue-collar district south of Baltimore, the other a liberal from the Washington suburbs and the state's wealthiest district. Caruso sought reactions to the expected amendment to extend the statute of limitations to 25 years and hoped he might come away with commitments to the four-year extension in the Senate-passed bill. The Baltimore-area moderate—a Greek Orthodox, pharmacist, and House veteran—listened to Caruso's pitch as he sorted through mail that had accumulated over the weekend. He seemed comfortable with what he heard but offered only that he didn't think the feared amendment would materialize. It was clear he would not commit—not yet, anyway. Still, Caruso felt confident that the delegate would be in the Conference's camp when the committee voted; but for his votes on the death penalty, he'd always been there for the Maryland Catholic Conference in the past.

The liberal was at her desk in her cramped delegate's office when Caruso arrived unannounced. A copy of the Baltimore Archdiocese's newspaper, the *Catholic Review*, was open in front of her. She is a Catholic, practices family law, and was in the first year of her first term as a state lawmaker. Caruso had spoken with her earlier in the session, but not at length. She told him that she had just read some of his quotes in the Catholic paper. Caruso's cited comments were in reaction to separate measures passed over the Conference's objections early the preceding week by the full House. A bill to permit pharmacists to dispense sometimes abortifacient "emergency contraceptives" had been approved by a one-vote margin. Caruso had characterized proponents as insensitive to parents who "would have no idea that their daughter would be going into a pharmacy and getting these pills without even seeing a doctor." "Parents should be scratching their heads right now," he had said, "wondering how on earth the House of Delegates could have approved this bill." Of a measure designed to compel Catholic Charities programs and other agencies engaging in state procurement contracts to hire persons engaged in homosexual lifestyles, Caruso was quoted as saying, "We should not have to cast our mission aside in order to do business with the state. . . . We respect people whose beliefs differ from ours; we ask the same treatment from the state."[43] (Although he was not quoted in the press, Dick Dowling said of the two House outcomes, "We had our butts handed to us." But the Conference rebounded, and several days after the House votes, the two bills were killed by a Senate committee.)

In her conversation with Caruso, the delegate unveiled her Catholic credentials, including service on the board of the Washington-area Catholic high school that she and her seven siblings had attended. Her father, she told Caruso, had been the school's principal. Sheepishly, she said, "We didn't help you much last week." She confessed she wasn't aware of the full implications of the procurement bill until she read the *Catholic Review* and acknowledged that on bills that hadn't passed through her committee, she sometimes relied for guidance on respected colleagues. Here, she admitted, she wasn't aware of the nuances. In contrast, the delegate offered no apology for her vote on emergency contraception, or for an earlier vote on a Maryland Catholic Conference budget amendment that sought to limit the expenditure of state Medicaid funds for abortions.

When the conversation turned to the child-abuse legislation, Caruso found the delegate generally sympathetic to the Conference's position. She suggested that a bill pending action by her committee, designed to reduce the statute of limitations in medical malpractice cases, might help advance the Conference's argument. Speaking as a practicing attorney, she said that the statute of limitations should be applied consistently; exceptions shouldn't be carved out for specific types of cases. The delegate recalled the case of an area football coach who was accused by men in their 30s of having sexually

abused them when they were teenagers. "How, at that point, can you
really know what happened?" she asked rhetorically. When Caruso
departed, he was confident the Washington-area delegate would oppose the feared amendment, though he worried that her interest in
the consistent application of the statute of limitations might cause her
to vote against the Senate-passed, four-year extension the Conference
was supporting.

The Judiciary Committee voted several days later. In the meantime,
Dowling waged an all-out assault on the amendment, shored up support for the Senate-passed measure, and, with Caruso and other
staffers, counted votes. Just prior to the voting session, Dowling told
the committee's chairman, a Catholic who regularly supported Maryland Catholic Conference positions, that there were sufficient votes to
kill the amendment and approve the bill. The two delegates with
whom Caruso had spoken in my presence joined the solid majority
that rejected their colleague's amendment. The moderate pharmacist
also joined the majority when the Senate-passed bill was approved 14
to 9. The Catholic liberal, true to her lawyer's conviction, voted
against its four-year statute of limitations extension. The committee-
approved measure would later pass the full House (139 to 1) and be
signed into law by Maryland's governor.

Following our Monday evening visits, I asked Jeff Caruso about his
approach to Catholic lawmakers whose votes on life-related issues,
like those of the Washington-area delegate, so often conflict with
church teaching. There are probably hundreds of such state legislators across the country: Catholics who are sympathetic to many of
their bishops' public policy priorities, but who are also decidedly pro-
choice. The issue was raised anew by a 2003 doctrinal note issued by
the Congregation for the Doctrine of the Faith "on some questions regarding the participation of Catholics in political life." The note reiterated the church's teaching on a variety of issues, including abortion,
and insists that "a well-formed Christian conscience does not permit
one to vote for a political program or an individual law which con-
tradicts the fundamental contents of faith and morals."[44]

I asked whether the doctrinal instruction affected Caruso's approach to such lawmakers. "First," said Caruso, "most of these people
would probably vote our way if they knew they could do so and still
get elected. Certainly not all of them, but most. It's no secret that
we've failed to generate sufficient support in the *Catholic* electorate,

let alone the general population, for candidates who abide the church's abortion teaching. I think the tide's changing—too slowly for my colleagues and me, but changing, nonetheless. Once it turns emphatically, we'll see a change in the way policymakers vote on the abortion issue." He continued, "At least some of our failure is attributable to our clergy. It's the clergy's job to inform our consciences, and part of that responsibility has to do with connecting the dots between church teaching and the issues that are being debated in the public forum. It's their job to exhort the faithful to be active citizens and voters and, in those capacities, to make that vital connection. Sadly, in too many of our parishes, that's just not getting done." Caruso focused on his role in dealing with Catholic policy makers who vote against pro-life measures: "My job is to present persuasive arguments on specific pieces of legislation. That includes changing the hearts and minds of people who disagree with our positions, but it doesn't include reminding them of their moral and spiritual obligations. Again, that's the job of clergy and church leaders. My challenge is to win, and that requires that I establish and maintain cordial working relationships with all legislators. Failure to do so could cause serious harm to the people who rely on our efforts in so many important policy areas."

As the hour for reconvening drew near, legislators began to make their way from their offices to the House and Senate chambers. Although there is an underground passage from the legislative office buildings to the statehouse, a passage that would have been particularly useful on that cold night, most legislators made the ceremonial walk outside, up the capitol steps and through the crowded lobby. As Dick Dowling stood at the foot of the capitol steps, nearly every legislator who passed by greeted him, including one who said with thick sarcasm and a smile, "Something important must be going on tonight," drawing out *im-por-tant* for emphasis. After nearly 20 years as an advocate in Annapolis, Dowling is an established figure in the legislative community. Over the years, he has developed the kind of relationship with some legislators that allows him to be the source or butt of jokes—and the kind of relationship that allows him at times to transcend the need to actively plead his case. Dowling might just step outside with a legislator during a break to smoke a cigarette and mention in passing, "I know you'll do the right thing."

At the stroke of midnight a week later, on schedule, the Maryland General Assembly's 2004 session adjourned *sine die*. There had been speculation that a special session might be needed to abide the state constitution's balanced-budget requirement, but that concern had been put to rest once potions whose magical ingredients are known only to government budget analysts had been applied. According to a Maryland Catholic Conference after-session report, "more than six percent of the 2,000 measures considered during the session (about 125) related to Church interests. Their progress was monitored by [Conference staffers]. On about half, the Conference took formal positions."[45] The outcomes of bills on which the Conference focused the greater portion of its advocacy attention were mixed. The enactment of the statute of limitations bill and the defeat of the measure that would have constricted the sacramental seal were clear victories. Cardinal Keeler wrote to Dowling on the session's final day, conveying congratulations, "It must be a great consolation to you to see that your argumentation, grounded in the faith and in the law, proved to be so effective." Cardinal McCarrick echoed the sentiment: "I would not have put money on our being able to get through this session unscathed, and yet, through your generalship and the relations that you have so carefully built up in Annapolis over the past many years, you did just that. You certainly are one of the best in the business and I congratulate you with great joy."

And there were other victories. At the Conference's urging, lawmakers approved a fiscal 2004 increase in cash-assistance grants to families on welfare (state budget analysts had recommended against doing so) and agreed to continue indefinitely a $34-million-a-year commitment to the Electric Universal Service Program for low-income households. Legislation to grant in-state tuition rates to children of undocumented immigrants who attend state colleges was enacted (though later vetoed by the governor). The House-passed bills related to state procurement contracts and the over-the-counter dispensing of emergency contraception were defeated in the Senate. A House panel rejected a measure to legitimate embryonic stem cell research and human cloning, following Maryland Catholic Conference–organized testimony that included presentations by representatives of the U.S. bishops conference and the President's Council on Bioethics. The same House panel spurned a bill to require poor people to sign health care advance directives as a condition for Medicaid coverage. And while funding for most state programs was cut, support for most anti-poverty programs was preserved and in a few cases (notably assisted-living, developmental-disabilities, and legal-assistance programs) increased.

There were some disappointments, as well. Bills calling for a two-year moratorium on state executions and a higher standard of proof in the sentencing phase of death-penalty proceedings were rejected by the full Senate (the moratorium measure by a single vote). Facing sure defeat in a House committee, a bill to enhance a parent's rights in the abortion decision of a minor daughter was withdrawn by its sponsor. Amendments to limit state Medicaid abortion funding to the circumstances covered by federal Medicaid law (*viz.*, life of the mother, rape, and incest) were defeated on the floors of both chambers, and a Senate chairman prevented a vote by her committee colleagues on legislation to expand the embrace of Maryland State Teacher Scholarships to nonpublic school teachers.

Some outcomes were neither defeats nor clear victories. Funding for the textbook-loan program was reduced by $750,000, but House and Senate amendments to cut the funding altogether were rejected, and voting for the approved $3 million authorization exhibited stronger lawmaker support than the program had received for its first three years of operation. And, although Conference-supported legislation to permit undocumented immigrants to hold Maryland driver's licenses was rejected, lawmakers did create a task force that will consider the sorts of documentation the state should require before granting licenses to such immigrants.

Examining the pattern of these legislative outcomes makes clear that Maryland Catholic Conference advocacy is just one of many factors involved in policy making in the Maryland General Assembly. The makeup of the executive and legislative branches creates a political opportunity structure that heavily conditions what the Conference hopes to achieve and how they go about their work. Most notably, Maryland politics has for decades been dominated by the Democratic Party. The General Assembly consists of 131 Democrats and only 57 Republicans, even after Republicans gained nine seats in the 2002 election. In that same election, Robert Ehrlich defeated Kathleen Kennedy Townsend, becoming the first Republican governor in Maryland since Spiro Agnew was elected in 1966. This Democratic dominance means that on two of its most important issues, abortion and Catholic schools, the Maryland Catholic Conference has only hoped for incremental positive changes and otherwise plays a lot of defense. It also affects the way they frame their issues. The legislation allowing pharmacists to dispense emergency contraception without a physician's approval is not a "pro-life" issue; it is a "pro-health" issue. According to Jeff Caruso, given the political realities of Maryland, "if this is seen as a life issue, we lose." The Conference's education strategy is "Count Us In." "Ours is not an anti–public school position," Mary Ellen Russell argues. "Eighty percent of Catholic students attend public schools. We are pro-inclusion for nonpublic school students."

The Republican Party's recent inroads raise the Maryland Catholic Conference's expectations in certain areas. As Dowling commented after the 2002 elections, "I think the new legislature will be markedly more pro-life than the current one. It's pretty clear that Governor Ehrlich will be more open to our anti-abortion agenda than Mrs. Townsend would have been had she been elected." On education issues, Dowling adds, "I think [Ehrlich] appears to us to be open to the prospect of broadening support for nonpublic schools." On the other hand, Ehrlich "promises to be more disposed to the death penalty" than Townsend would have been, and "it remains to be seen how committed he will be to the anti-poverty social justice programs we care so much about." Perhaps the most hopeful sign for the Maryland Catholic Conference is the election of Ehrlich's running mate, Lieutenant Governor Michael Steele, whom Dowling characterizes as "a person who was born and raised in the Church, attended Catholic schools, is strongly pro-life, strongly anti–death penalty and shares the Church's concern for the poor and vulnerable."[46] He is what the late Joseph Cardinal Bernardin would call a "consistent life ethic" Catholic, or what John Paul II would call a "well-formed" Catholic.

But for every Michael Steele in politics, there are a dozen who do not support the church's nonpartisan agenda. Considering four issues of interest to the Maryland Catholic Conference that received floor votes in both the Senate and House of Delegates in 2003—abortion funding, textbook funding, immigrant tuition, and energy assistance— only 13 of 188 legislators (6.9 percent) supported the Maryland Catholic Conference's position in every vote, including about equal proportions of Democrats (7.6 percent) and Republicans (5.3 percent).[47] Of course, it is possible to see this political glass as half full rather than half empty: No legislator voted against the Conference's preferred position on every issue. Having a nonpartisan agenda in a partisan political system can be an advantage, at times. The Maryland

Catholic Conference staff has relationships with legislators in both parties that other interest groups do not. Their pro-life advocacy gives them access to some more-conservative legislators that liberal interest groups do not have, and their advocacy on behalf of the poor gives them access to some more-liberal legislators that conservative interest groups do not have. "No matter the legislator—right or left, Democrat or Republican—we look for common ground," says Jeff Caruso. "Our best friend one day might be our fiercest opponent the next. This enables an across-the-board access that few other groups enjoy." The staff also maintains interest group relationships that cut across the left/right ideological divide. The Conference is the leading member of a coalition opposing the death penalty and the leading member of the coalition that supports limitations on abortion. Tellingly, at one point during the 2003 session, members of the anti–death penalty group were gathered around the Conference's conference table while, in an adjoining room, Caruso and Nancy Fortier plotted strategy to defeat the emergency-contraception bill, a measure supported by most of the organizations represented at the conference table.

This description of the Maryland Catholic Conference offers an excellent overview of the scale, scope, and style of advocacy by state Catholic conferences today. This is not to say that the Maryland Catholic Conference is the norm. A survey of other conference directors, in fact, reveals it to be one of the best conferences. At the same time, as the following chapters will show, the Maryland Catholic Conference is in many ways typical. Its dual structure of bishops as the board of directors and professional lay people staffing the secretariat, its "seamless garment" of legislative priorities held together by a defense of human dignity, and its deep involvement in the details of legislative "sausage-making" are all par for the course in contemporary state Catholic conferences. As the balance of this book will show, it is how Catholic bishops engage in state politics today.

NOTES

1. This chapter is a selective historical overview that seeks to highlight some of the important developments in the Catholic Church's public engagement in the United States over the past three-plus centuries. For more comprehensive historical studies, see Jay Dolan, *The American Catholic*

Experience: A History from Colonial Times to the Present (Garden City, NY: Doubleday, 1985); James Hennesey, S.J., *American Catholics: A History of the Roman Catholic Community in the United States* (New York: Oxford University Press, 1981); John McGreevy, *Catholicism and American Freedom: A History* (New York: W.W. Norton, 2003); and Charles Morris, *American Catholic* (New York: Times Books, 1997).

The historical overview of Maryland is reconstructed from various sources, including Timothy Byrnes, *Catholic Bishops in American Politics* (Princeton, NJ: Princeton University Press, 1991); Chester Gillis, *Roman Catholicism in America* (New York: Columbia University Press, 1999); Thomas O'Brien Hanley, S.J., *Their Rights and Liberties: The Beginnings of Religious and Political Freedom in Maryland* (Westminster, MD: The Newman Press, 1959); and Richard Walsh and William Lloyd Fox, eds., *Maryland: A History, 1632–1974* (Baltimore, MD: Maryland Historical Society, 1974).

There are many locations and points in time at which one can begin to tell the story of the Catholic Church in America. In focusing on Maryland, I do not wish to suggest that the history of Catholicism in the United States began with the British colonies. Rather, I highlight the fact that the seeds of the church *hierarchy*—my main concern here—were planted at St. Mary's City in the Maryland Colony through the efforts of the Calvert family. Obviously, a complete history of the church in America would have to take account of Spanish and French exploration of the "New World." The first Mass celebrated in America is believed to have taken place at St. Augustine (Florida) on February 8, 1565, the site of the oldest American parish. In the seventeenth and eighteenth centuries, Spanish Franciscans and Jesuits were active as missionaries in the West and Southwest (Texas, New Mexico, Arizona, California), and French Jesuits in the Mississippi Valley and upper Midwest. See, e.g., James Fischer, *Catholics in America* (New York: Oxford University Press, 2000), chapter 1; Dolan, *The American Catholic Experience*, chapter 1.

2. Quoted in Hanley, *Their Rights and Liberties*, pp. 77–78.

3. Andrew White, S.J., "Voyage to Maryland" (*Relatio Itineris in Marilandiam*), trans. and ed. Barbara Lawatsch-Boomgaarden (Wauconda, IL: Bolchazy-Carducci Publishers, 1995), p. 35. In 1916, the Maryland General Assembly authorized "Maryland Day" (March 25) as a legal holiday in the state.

4. Henry Browne, "Catholicism in the United States," in James Ward Smith and A. Leland Jamison, eds., *The Shaping of American Religion* (Princeton, NJ: Princeton University Press, 1961), p. 78.

5. Patrick Carey, *The Roman Catholics* (Westport, CT: Greenwood Press, 1993), p. 21.

6. Hanley, *Their Rights and Liberties*, p. 120.

7. "To Charles Carroll of Carrollton," in Thomas O'Brien Hanley, S.J., ed., *The John Carroll Papers, Volume 1: 1755–1791* (Notre Dame, IN: University

of Notre Dame Press, 1976), p. 82. This letter is well-known among Catholic historians and is cited in Annabelle Melville, *John Carroll of Baltimore: Founder of the American Catholic Hierarchy* (New York: Charles Scribner's Sons, 1955), p. 56; and James Hennesey, S.J., "Roman Catholics and American Politics, 1900–1960: Altered Circumstances, Continuing Patterns," pp. 302–21 in Mark Noll, ed., *Religions and American Politics: From the Colonial Period to the 1980s* (New York: Oxford University Press, 1990), p. 308.

8. "Powerhouse" is from Eric Hanson, *The Catholic Church in World Politics* (Princeton: Princeton University Press, 1987), p. 167. More generally, see Byrnes, *Catholic Bishops in American Politics*, pp. 12–17.

9. Michael P. Young, "Confessional Protest: The Religious Birth of U.S. National Social Movements," *American Sociological Review* 67 (October 2002): 660–688.

10. Jose Casanova, *Public Religions in the Modern World* (Chicago: University of Chicago Press, 1994), p. 179.

11. Byrnes, *Catholic Bishops in American Politics*, p. 12.

12. John Paul II, *Apostolos Suos* ("On the Theological and Juridical Nature of Episcopal Conferences"), Apostolic Letter *Motu Proprio*, 21 May 1998, no. 3.

13. *Apostolos Suos*, no. 4. See also the analysis in Joseph Komonchak, "On the Authority of the Bishops' Conferences," *America* (September 12, 1998), p. 7.

14. Thomas Reese, S.J., *A Flock of Shepherds: The National Conference of Catholic Bishops* (Kansas City, MO: Sheed & Ward, 1992), p. 21.

15. *Apostolos Suos*, no. 4.

16. Joseph Komonchak, "Introduction: Episcopal Conferences Under Criticism," pp. 1–22 in Thomas Reese, ed., *Episcopal Conferences: Historical, Canonical, and Theological Studies* (Washington, DC: Georgetown University Press, 1989), pp. 1, 2.

17. James Hennesey, S.J., "Councils in America," in *A National Pastoral Council: Pro and Con* (Washington, DC: United States Catholic Conference, 1971), p. 39; Jay Dolan, *Catholic Revivalism: The American Experience, 1830–1900* (Notre Dame, IN: University of Notre Dame Press, 1978), pp. 30–31; Reese, *A Flock of Shepherds*, p. 362n12; Gerald Fogarty, S.J., *The Vatican and the American Hierarchy from 1870 to 1965* (Wilmington, DE: Michael Glazier, 1985); Elizabeth McKeown, "The National Bishops' Conference: An Analysis of Its Origins," *Catholic Historical Review* 66 (October 1980): 570.

18. See Allen Hertzke, *Representing God in Washington: The Role of Religious Lobbies in the American Polity* (Knoxville, TN: University of Tennessee Press, 1988).

19. Michael Zöller, *Washington and Rome: Catholicism in American Culture* (Notre Dame, IN: University of Notre Dame Press, 1999), p. 156. Interestingly, Zöller notes that "the most striking institutional growth occurs in the

number of dioceses, which increased from 23 archdioceses and 102 dioceses in 1950 to 36 archdioceses and 162 dioceses in 1993. This increase by more than half is significantly greater than the increase in the number of parishes, which grew from 15,000 to 20,000 over the same period" (p. 191).

20. Elizabeth McKeown, "The 'National Idea' in the History of the American Episcopal Conference," pp. 59–84 in Reese, ed., *Episcopal Conferences*, p. 64.

21. McKeown, "The National Bishops' Conference," p. 569.

22. McKeown, "The 'National Idea,'" pp. 66–67.

23. There was also an ideological dimension to the dissent. According to Thomas Reese, "The Rev. John Ryan, director of the council's new department of social action, further alienated conservative elements with his advocacy of liberal labor policies. Father Ryan's 'Program of Social Reconstruction,' issued by the four-member Administrative Committee of the War Council, became widely identified with the whole American hierarchy and known simply as 'The Bishops' Program'" (Reese, *A Flock of Shepherds*, p. 24).

24. McKeown, "The National Bishops' Conference," pp. 581–83; Gerald Fogarty, S.J., "The Authority of the National Catholic Welfare Council," pp. 85–103 in Reese, ed., *Episcopal Conferences*, pp. 90–93.

25. From an interview quoted in Reese, *A Flock of Shepherds*, p. 27.

26. *Pastoral Letters of the United States Catholic Bishops*, 4 vols., 1792–1983 (Washington, DC: United States Catholic Conference, 1984).

27. McKeown, "The 'National Idea,'" p. 83.

28. Mary Hanna, "Bishops as Political Leaders," pp. 75–86 in Charles Dunn, ed., *Religion in American Politics* (Washington, DC: Congressional Quarterly Press, 1989), p. 76.

29. John McGreevy, "Catholics and Civic Engagement in the United States," Spring 2000 Joint Consultation, Commonweal Foundation and Faith & Reason Institute, 2–4 June 2000. See also J. Bryan Hehir, "The Church in the World: Responding to the Call of the Council," pp. 101–19 in James Heft, S.M., ed., *Faith and the Intellectual Life: Marianist Award Lectures* (Notre Dame, IN: University of Notre Dame Press, 1996), p. 114.

30. Jay Dolan, *In Search of an American Catholicism* (New York: Oxford University Press, 2002), p. 194.

31. Jose Casanova, *Public Religions in the Modern World*, pp. 72–73, and chapter 7 on Catholicism in the United States generally. Casanova also considers *Lumen Gentium* ("Dogmatic Constitution on the Church"), which he argues "radically altered the self-identity of the church as a religious institution by placing at the beginning of the text the definition of the church as 'the People of God'" (p. 73). In my view, this document—as important as it is to the inner workings of the church—is less important in setting the context for the work of state Catholic conferences than *Gaudium et Spes* or *Dignitatis Humanae*.

32. Casanova, *Public Religions*, pp. 72–73.

33. Pope Paul VI, *Ecclesiae Sanctae*, Apostolic Letter *Motu Proprio*, 6 August 1966.

34. Reese, *A Flock of Shepherds*, p. 30.

35. Fogarty, "The Authority of the National Catholic Welfare Council," p. 102.

36. Zöller, *Washington and Rome*, p. 193.

37. The fact that two of the three dioceses served by the Maryland Catholic Conference cross state lines is unique among state Catholic conferences. The five Maryland counties that are part of the Archdiocese of Washington are home to 42 percent of Maryland's Catholics, and the Eastern Shore of Maryland in the Diocese of Wilmington is home to only about 3 percent of Maryland's Catholics. The rest live in the Archdiocese of Baltimore.

38. "Former Jurist, State Senator is New Board Member," *Conference Call: The Newsletter of the Maryland Catholic Conference*, January 2003, p. 3.

39. "About the Maryland Catholic Conference," *Conference Call: The Newsletter of the Maryland Catholic Conference*, Winter 2002, p. 4.

40. *Building Blocks for Catholic Advocacy: Public Policy Initiatives of the Maryland Catholic Conference, 2003–2006* (Annapolis, MD: Maryland Catholic Conference, n.d.), p. 8.

41. McCarrick, "Some Things One Cannot Do," *Catholic Standard*, 20 February 2003; "McCarrick Decries Md. Child Abuse Bill," *Washington Post*, 20 February 2003, pp. B1, B10; "Md. Panel Rejects Child Abuse Bill After Uproar," *Washington Post*, 1 March 2003.

42. "Forcing Disclosure of Abuse Debated," *Baltimore Sun*, 26 February 2003, pp. 1B, 9B; "Child-Abuse Victims' Bill Advances in Senate," *Washington Post*, 20 March 2003.

43. "Maryland Catholic Conference has a Mixed Week in Annapolis," *Catholic Review*, 27 March 2003; "Catholic Social Services Threatened," *Catholic Review*, 27 March 2003.

44. Congregation for the Doctrine of the Faith, "Doctrinal Note on Some Questions Regarding the Participation of Catholics in Political Life," issued 16 January 2003, quote from no. 4.

45. *MCC in 2003* (Annapolis: Maryland Catholic Conference, 2003), p. 3.

46. "Ehrlich Administration Expected to Address Key Catholic Issues," *Catholic Review*, 14 November 2002; "After Election Surprises in Maryland, Impact of Budget Cuts among Key Issues," *Catholic Standard*, 14 November 2002.

47. Calculated from the end-of-year legislative "scorecard" produced by the Maryland Catholic Conference for publication in the Catholic newspapers serving Maryland.

2

Organization

State Catholic Conferences as Dual Structures

This chapter addresses state Catholic conferences from an organizational perspective, examining the ecology of their establishment, budgets and staff size, raison d'être, and especially their "dual" structure. It takes as its point of departure an analysis of state Catholic conferences written in 1971 by Rev. Michael J. Sheehan. *The State Catholic Conference: A New Development in Intereccle-sial Cooperation in the United States* was Sheehan's doctoral dissertation in canon law, and, as the subtitle suggests, the subject matter at the time was novel.[1]* Indeed, at the time Sheehan was conducting his research in 1970, the median age of state Catholic conferences was just three years.

That Sheehan's study has aged remarkably well over the past three decades is a testament to his insight. Of course, in some small ways the document shows its age. At one point Sheehan refers to "office girls" at the conferences (p. 29), but for the most part the study retains its relevance and provides an excellent benchmark against which to compare today's state conferences. As table 2.1 documents, the youthful organizations that Sheehan studied 30 years ago have multiplied and aged (see also table A.1 in appendix A for the exact years of establishment for the 34 existing conferences). Thus, this chapter

---

*Citations to Sheehan's dissertation will henceforward be given parenthetically in the text. See note 1 for the full citation.

Table 2.1. Number and Average Age of State Catholic Conferences, 1970 and 2002

	1970	2002
Number of Conferences	22	34
Mean Age (Years)	6	32
Median Age (Years)	3	34

offers insight into the similarities, differences, and patterns of evolution of state Catholic conferences over this time period.[2] It also goes beyond Sheehan's description by sociologically analyzing the *dual structure* of state Catholic conferences and pointing to the implications of this for their political advocacy.

STATE CATHOLIC CONFERENCES DEFINED

Sheehan's 1971 definition still captures the essence of what state Catholic conferences are and do:

> A State Catholic Conference is a permanent, non-canonical Church agency, composed of the dioceses within a state to provide the coordination of the Church's public policy and communication with state government, non-Catholic Churches and secular agencies. The bishops of the state form the board of directors and set the policy. Laymen, priests and religious are often members of the board as well, or at least have some consultative role. There is a secretariat, located in the state capital, and usually headed by a lay executive director. Experts in various fields compose the departments of the Conferences and handle matters such as the Catholic schools, hospitals, charitable institutions, ecumenical relations, public information and civil legal affairs. The State Conferences closely resemble, on the state level, the United States Catholic Conference on the national level. Each Conference is somewhat different from the other, tailored to fit the needs of the Church in a particular state. (p. 79)

As non-canonical entities, the authority of state Catholic conferences is far more limited than the United States Conference of Catholic Bishops (USCCB).[3] At the same time, in terms of its extra-ecclesial activities, it is very appropriate to view state Catholic conferences as the functional equivalents of the USCCB in the states.

ECOLOGY: THE ESTABLISHMENT
OF STATE CATHOLIC CONFERENCES

Of the origins of state Catholic conferences, Sheehan writes, "There is no law which bids the bishops to come together but the law of love of Christ's Church." In his view, an awareness of the need for interecclesial communion moves the bishops to organize conferences (p. 42). At the same time, as we will see, there are mundane factors beyond the "love of Christ's Church" that drive the awareness of a need to establish state Catholic conferences.

In 1970, the bishops in 22 of 50 states had established conferences. In explaining the difference between those states with and without a conference, Sheehan focused on the number of dioceses in the state. He concluded, "When there is only one diocese in a state there is not as much difficulty in communications and many things can be organized through the one chancery office in the state, whereas when there are several dioceses the need for an agency through which the Church state-wide might communicate is much greater" (p. 22). Table 2.2 shows the considerable difference in the number of dioceses in those states with and without established conferences, a gap that existed in 1970 and grew by 2002.

When Sheehan was writing in 1970, three states—California, Louisiana, and Alaska—had three or more dioceses but no conference. Not surprisingly, the bishops of these states established conferences soon after Sheehan completed his work: both California and

Table 2.2. Comparison of Average Number of Dioceses in States with and without Established Catholic Conferences in 1970 and 2002

Year	Conference Established	No Conference Established	Total Number of Dioceses
1970	4.33	1.81	151
2002	4.41	1.47	175

Note: For purposes of comparison, this table includes only Latin Rite dioceses. It does not include Eastern Rite eparchies in the United States, even though in some cases they are represented by state Catholic conferences. There are 17 Eastern Rite eparchies in the United States, but only 8 of them formally participate on the boards of state Catholic conferences, including: the Ukranian Eparchy of Stamford (Connecticut Catholic Conference); the Byzantine Eparchy of Passaic and Our Lady of Deliverance Syriac Catholic Diocese (New Jersey Catholic Conference); the Byzantine Eparchy of Parma, Romanian Catholic Diocese of Canton, and Ukranian Catholic Diocese of Parma (Catholic Conference of Ohio); and the Philadelphia Ukrainian Catholic Archeparchy and Pittsburgh Byzantine Catholic Archdiocese (Pennsylvania Catholic Conference).

Louisiana in 1972, and Alaska in 1973. Of the 12 states—including the District of Columbia—that have established conferences since 1970, three have only one diocese: West Virginia, Hawaii, and Washington, D.C. Sheehan points out that "even one-diocese-states need a means of communication with the various branches of state government and secular groups" (p. 24). Although these three states have opted to form a conference, this need could also be fulfilled by a diocesan office (as in Utah, South Dakota, Maine, and elsewhere) or a contract lobbyist (as in Delaware).

Thus, the number of dioceses is an important but not the only factor in understanding the establishment of state Catholic conferences. We can further understand the difference between the states with state Catholic conferences and those without by examining the varying size of the Catholic population across the states. Looking only at those states with either two or three dioceses, we find that states with state Catholic conferences have on average 392,762 Catholics in the population and a 16 percent share of the total population. States with two or three dioceses but no state Catholic conferences, by contrast, average considerably fewer Catholics in the population (232,559), and a much smaller proportion of the state population are Catholics (6.9 percent).

Table A.2 in appendix A gives the Catholic characteristics of the 17 states with no state Catholic conference in 2002. Based on this demographic data, if I were to try to predict which states would be the next to establish conferences, I would look to South Dakota with its high percentage of Catholics in the state population (21.5 percent)—even though the total number of Catholics in the state is small (156,727)—and especially to Virginia with its large number of Catholics (553,709)—even though the percentage of Catholics is somewhat small (8 percent). Even at 8 percent Catholic, Virginia has twice the percentage of Catholics as the other Southern states with at least two dioceses and no state Catholic conference (Alabama, Mississippi, North Carolina, and Tennessee).

Demographic and theological differences between the Diocese of Arlington and the Diocese of Richmond have thus far prevented the establishment of a conference in Virginia. Although it was only created in 1974, almost two-thirds of the Catholics in Virginia (63.8 percent) live in the Diocese of Arlington. The Arlington Diocese is largely constituted by the Washington, D.C., suburbs, which are populated by transplants from other parts of the country who are working in government or industry in the national capital area. Catholics are only 8 percent of the total population in Virginia, but they are 15.2 percent of the population in the Arlington Diocese. In contrast, the Diocese of Richmond encompasses the vast area of central and southern Virginia, which includes some urban areas (Richmond, Hampton Roads-Virginia Beach) but also many rural areas. Catholics are only 4.3 percent of the population in the Richmond Diocese. On top of these demographic differences are theological differences in the administration of the two dioceses. Bishop Paul Loverde of Arlington, appointed by Pope John Paul II, is known as one of the most conservative bishops in the United States, and Bishop Walter Sullivan—appointed auxiliary bishop of Richmond in 1970 by Paul VI, promoted to bishop in 1974, and now retired—is known as one of the more liberal. For some time, the two only communicated with one another through third parties.[4] In 2002, Bishop Sullivan petitioned the Vatican to split his diocese in two, creating a new diocese centered in Virginia Beach in the southeastern part of the state. If this split is approved, the Commonwealth of Virginia would have over half a million Catholics spread over three dioceses. This might force the bishops of Virginia to contemplate seriously the founding of a conference, a move that could be facilitated by Sullivan's retirement in 2003.[5]

Sometimes seemingly anomalous cases merit attention because they are exceptions that help to prove the rule. Rhode Island is such a case here. With its 623,752 Catholics who are 63.1 percent of the total state population, Rhode Island would seem more likely to have a state Catholic conference than other one-diocese states like Hawaii (124,987 population and 10.5 percent population share) or West Virginia (97,232 population and 5.3 percent population share). Although the Diocese of Providence is represented in the public policy arena by its governmental liaison, Rev. Bernard A. Healey, at nearly two-thirds of the population the church in Rhode Island need not be as organized for advocacy as in other states, at least not yet. As Brown University political scientist Darrell West commented to the Associated Press, "When you have such a large number of Catholics, the distinction between church and state disappears for all practical purposes."[6] A similar situation obtains with respect to the Church of Christ of Latter-day Saints in Mormon-dominated Utah.

GROWTH: BUDGETS AND STAFF SIZE[7]

Sheehan argues that it may be fiscally prohibitive for a one-diocese state to establish a conference. He considers the example of Wyoming, with 45,000 Catholics in the entire state in 1970 (just over 14 percent of the population), and concludes that "the Bishop of Cheyenne might find that the $30,000 or more that it would cost to set up a Conference would be more than he could afford to provide" (p. 24). Adjusted for inflation, the cost of a conference today would seem to be even more prohibitive, especially considering that in 2001 there were still only 48,781 Catholics in Wyoming, slightly more than 10 percent of the state population.

Although staffs and budgets have grown, on average, over the past 30 years, the start-up costs of establishing a conference are not as great as might be expected. The smallest conference budget in 1970 was $29,000, which adjusted for inflation would be $134,560 in 2002 (table 2.3). In fact, the smallest budget in 2002 was $22,000, *less* than the smallest budget in 1970. Two of the most recently established conferences—New Mexico (est. 1991) and Nevada (est. 2000)—have among the smallest budgets, and this is achieved largely by employing a minimal staff. In 2002, both of the executive directors, Juan Montoya of New Mexico and V. Robert Payant of

Table 2.3. State Catholic Conference Budgets, 1970 and 2002

	Actual 1970 Budget	Inflation Adjusted 1970 Budget	Actual 2002 Budget
Smallest	$29,000	$134,560	$22,000
Largest	$300,000	$1,392,000	$1,300,000
Average	$95,152	$441,505	$402,659
	Actual 1970 Per Capita Budget	Inflation Adjusted 1970 Per Capita Budget	Actual 2002 Per Capita Budget
Smallest	$0.026	$0.12	$0.046
Largest	$0.275	$1.30	$1.14
Average	$0.108	$0.51	$0.36

Notes: 1970 budget data are from a survey of state Catholic conferences conducted by Mr. Ronald Hayes, executive director of the Colorado Catholic Conference, dated 11 August 1970. Inflation adjustment is based on CPI calculator provided by the U.S. Bureau of Labor Statistics, Division of Consumer Prices and Price Indexes (www.bls.gov/cpi), where $1.00 in 1970 is equivalent to $4.64 in 2002.

Nevada, were part-time employees. Moreover, Payant is retired from his main profession, and so the salary he draws is even less than if he were in the job market full time. Clearly, if the bishop or bishops of a state decided that a conference was of value, they could certainly establish one for less than one dollar per Catholic in the state per year. While the average per-Catholic expenditure for state conferences is $0.36, the New Mexico Catholic Conference spends about $0.06, and the Nevada Catholic Conference spends just under $0.05 per Catholic per year.

Certainly, the cost of state Catholic conferences in general has increased over time. As table 2.3 shows, the average budget of conferences in 1970 was $95,152. By 2002, the average budget had increased to $402,659. But this increase in the average budget is less than what would be expected based on the rate of inflation over this period of time. The inflation-adjusted average is nearly 10 percent higher than the actual average in 2002. This is so despite the fact that technology has become more intensive and extensive in conference work. Sheehan noted in 1970 that "some of the larger Conferences have xerox machines" (p. 34). Today, photocopiers, computers and printers, fax machines, local area networks, and Internet connections—and the supplies and maintenance required to run them—are all *de rigueur* for political advocacy organizations. However, because conferences are funded by diocesan assessments ("taxes"), most conference directors are cautious not to overspend.

Technology notwithstanding, the major factor in the growth of state Catholic conference budgets is increases in staff size. Not surprisingly, the correlation between size of staff and budget is nearly perfect (Pearson's correlation coefficient [r] = 0.925, where 1.0 is a perfect correlation). The average state Catholic conference has about one more full-time staff member today than in 1970 (see table 2.4).

As table 2.4 demonstrates, the *mean* number of full-time employees (FTEs) increased by 0.86 over this time period. If we break this FTE increase down into its component parts, we find that the increase is due to an increase in full-time staff from 2.82 on average in 1970 to 3.86 in 2002. This increase in full-time staff is offset somewhat by a decrease in part-time staff (from 1.24 on average in 1970 to 0.89 in 2002), suggesting that as they mature state Catholic conferences are becoming more professionalized.

Table 2.4.   State Catholic Conference Staff, 1970 and 2002

	1970	*2002*
Total Staff (FTEs)		
Range	1 to 11	0.5 to 10.5
Mean	3.44	4.30
Full-Time Staff		
Range	0 to 10	0 to 10
Mean	2.82	3.86
Part-Time Staff		
Range	0 to 3	0 to 4
Mean	1.24	0.89

Note: In calculating the *total* number of staff ("full time equivalents" or FTEs), full time staff are counted as 1.0 and part time staff are counted as 0.5.

RAISON D' ÊTRE: PRINCIPALLY PUBLIC POLICY

When he summarizes the major achievements of state Catholic conferences as of 1970, Sheehan first points to various instances of successful "interecclesial cooperation." He gives the example of the Kansas Catholic Conference, which facilitated the discovery of "common grounds between the superintendents of schools, the directors of charities and the diocesan lawyers on matters which previously had been handled by individuals within the four dioceses of Kansas." The Catholic Conference of Ohio created a channel of communication between women religious in the state—with their concerns over schools and hospitals they sponsor and staff, and their religious communities in general—and the bishops (p. 48).

The same is true today. Every state Catholic conference dedicates at least some of its resources to fostering collaboration and communication between various church actors in the state. In fact, the median number of diocesan offices or agencies with which state conferences have regular contact is five. A good example that is near the high end of the range is the Catholic Conference of Ohio, whose staff meets at least twice a year with the heads of nine different offices or agencies. These include the superintendents of schools and the diocesan directors of religious education, campus ministry, social action, Catholic Charities, youth ministry, cemeteries, evangelization, and pro-life and family life. The most commonly named contacts among all state Catholic conferences are the diocesan attorneys and education departments, social justice and respect life committees, and Catholic Charities agencies.

It seems safe to say that no conference does more to coordinate the activities of the church at the state level than Texas. The executive director for the past 20-plus years, Brother Richard Daly, C.S.C., describes some of the Texas Catholic Conference's activities:

> We have 20 departments, and those are ministries which every diocese has, like Catholic schools superintendent, Director of Catholic Charities, and so on. And then we have affiliated organizations like rural life people, mission activity people, people who work with the Society for the Propagation of Faith, people who do home and foreign mission activities. We have a twinning project. The dioceses of Texas have twinned with the dioceses of Honduras and the people in our mission office are very involved in that. We have a state Catholic archive and a state historical society that publishes a historical journal called *Catholic Southwest*. And that all is done out of this office.

The Texas Catholic Conference's mission clearly states, "The primary purpose of the Conference is to encourage and foster cooperation and communication among the dioceses and the ministries of the Catholic Church in Texas." Daly notes that "the job description of the executive director says that a *secondary* but important function is public policy." This mission makes sense, given the size of the church in Texas—it has the third highest number of Catholics (over five million) and the most dioceses (15) of any state in the country—and the correspondingly large task of coordination.

At the same time, unlike the conferences in other large states such as New York and California, the Texas Catholic Conference staff has made a conscious choice to perform these services, and the bishops of the state have welcomed them. "The conference started out as strictly public policy 40 years ago," Daly recalls. "The first director was a former lobbyist, a former legislator, attorney, layman. But he and his successor saw the conference as more than just public policy, especially since the Texas legislature meets only every other year for 140 days. And 40 years ago that was really the case. There wasn't much government in Texas. So they saw the conference as being a vehicle to bring together all the ministries in the church of Texas, to be an umbrella organization for all of the dioceses, a vehicle of communication among the dioceses and the various ministries within the dioceses."

Thus, even the experience of Texas helps point to the fact that the political functions of state Catholic conferences have been dominant from the start.

In her canon law licentiate thesis, Dr. Marie Hilliard (who happens to be the executive director of the Connecticut Catholic Conference), states plainly, "State conferences developed due to the need to carry the Gospel imperatives into the public policy arena."[8] Thus, state Catholic conferences are best seen as an adaptation of the Catholic Church as an organization and religious tradition to the political and cultural realities of the United States. As Thomas Reese has noted of the activities of the National Conference of Catholic Bishops, "the shepherds cannot roam where they will; they are corralled by history, theology, and church law."[9] The same is true of the bishops of a particular state. The U.S. bishops conference has real (if limited) authority in the church to make decisions on liturgical matters (e.g., receiving communion standing and in the hand); religious practice (e.g., standards for fasting and abstinence); and discipline in the church (e.g., the recently implemented essential norms for dealing with allegations of sexual abuse of minors by priests or deacons)—in communion with the Holy See. In contrast, Hilliard observes that state conferences of bishops are "supra-diocesan structures without canonical status; they do not have a corporate legislative authority" in the church. "A state conference has no collective authority to exercise teaching or governing functions or to perform pastoral activities. The exercise of such functions and the performance of such pastoral activity is restricted to each diocesan bishop within his own territory."[10]

Unlike dioceses and nations, which have status under both civil and church law, states are exclusively civil constructions. It makes sense, therefore, that state conferences should act principally as civil organizations. The raison d'être of state Catholic conferences is principally to engage in the public policy process—or, more broadly, in the public life—of the state. Richard Daly's comment about the origins of the Texas Catholic Conference suggests as much. Similarly, Marie Hilliard observes that "the establishment of the Massachusetts Catholic Conference in 1969 was a direct result of the recognized need to impact public policy affecting diocesan Catholic Charities."[11]

This pattern of being publicly focused is born out in my survey of state conference directors in 2002, in which I replicated two questions Sheehan asked about the place of legislative politics in conference work. Respondents were asked, "In general, would you characterize your Conference's participation in state policy making as: a predominant concern; one of several concerns; or incidental to its regular business." A full 87.5 percent of conferences responded that state policy making was *a predominant concern*. Only 12.5 percent of conferences—including Connecticut, New Jersey, and Texas—responded that it was *one of several concerns*. A related question asked conferences to "rank from #1 to #5 the following groups to which the Conference should address itself, with #1 being the most important group and #5 being the least important group: state legislature, the Catholic Church within the state, other churches, nondenominational groups, and other." In this case, the *state legislature* was the top-ranked target to which conferences address themselves, with 78.1 percent of respondents ranking it #1. *The Catholic Church within the state* was a distant second, with 21.9 percent of respondents ranking it #1. Considering the responses to these two questions jointly, only two state Catholic conferences (including Texas, not surprisingly) indicated that the state legislature was one of several concerns (not the predominant concern) *and* that the Catholic Church within the state was the primary audience to which conferences should address themselves.[12]

Although no conference is exclusively involved in public policy, involvement in the policy-making process in the state legislative arena is the predominant concern of state Catholic conferences generally. Hence, the focus of this book is on these activities to the exclusion of the other good works they do for the church in their respective states.

In understanding the political advocacy of state Catholic conferences, the single most important organizational factor is their dual structure. In the balance of this chapter, therefore, I explain state conferences as dual structures and hint at the implications of this for their political legitimacy and practices.

ORGANIZATION: CATHOLIC CONFERENCES AS DUAL STRUCTURES

Like the United States Conference of Catholic Bishops after the merger of the National Conference of Catholic Bishops (NCCB) and the United States Catholic Conference (USCC), state Catholic conferences appear from the outside to be unitary organizational structures. Sociologically, however, it is useful to conceptualize them as dual structures. Most simply put, this dual structure is evident in the fact that the bishops of a state form the board of directors, and lay people generally staff the secretariat. This dual structure of bishops and staff is crucial to understanding the ability of state Catholic conferences to negotiate the competing demands of faith and political involvement.

I owe the concept of religious organizations as dual structures to sociologist Mark Chaves, who argues that denominations "are constituted by two parallel organizational structures: a religious authority structure and an agency structure" (see table 2.5). According to Chaves, "A religious authority structure *inside* a complex religious organization such as a denomination performs the basic function of controlling access to religious goods, however religious goods are identified by particular religious traditions."[13] Roman Catholicism, in fact, is one of the easiest denominations in which to see the authority structure. For sociologists from Max Weber to the present, it has been the very definition of a hierarchical religious organization, with bishops and clergy as the central authority figures.

To understand the distinction and relationship between authority and agency structures, Chaves looks to the name itself. *Agency* struc-

Table 2.5.   Religious Authority Structure vs. Agency Structure

	Authority Structure	Agency Structure
Definitional Characteristics		
Goal orientation	Internal/religious control	External/engagement with the world
Basis of differentiation	Geographical segmentation	Functional differentiation
Primary role	Clergy/bishop	Administrator
Basis of legitimate authority	Traditional/charismatic	Rational/legal
Application to Roman Catholicism in United States		
National-level	National Conference of Catholic Bishops (NCCB)	United States Catholic Conference (USCC)
State-level	Bishops as State Catholic Conference Board of Directors	SCC Professional Staff as Secretariat

Note: This table gives the original (1966) post-Vatican II organization of the national-level episcopal conference for illustrative purposes. In July 2001, the NCCB and the USCC were merged into a single organization, the United States Conference of Catholic Bishops (USCCB), thus internalizing the dual structure.

Source: Definitional characteristics are from Chaves, "Denominations as Dual Structures: An Organizational Analysis," *Sociology of Religion* 54 (1993), table 2, p. 157.

tures are "meant to function as the *agents* of the religious authority structure in the secular world, hence the nomenclature."[14] Examples include missions, social services, publishing, and, yes, political lobbying. The primary goal orientation of religious agency structures, then, is *external* (the world). Although the Vatican II "Pastoral Constitution on the Church in the Modern World" (*Gaudium et Spes*) teaches that the church properly seeks to engage the world, the primary orientation of the hierarchy is *internal*—religious control within the church. In Roman Catholicism, bishops are first and foremost "teachers of doctrine, priests of sacred worship, and officers of good order" in the church ("Dogmatic Constitution on the Church," *Lumen Gentium*, no. 20).

As table 2.5 indicates, the primary role in the authority structure is that of clergy or bishop, and in the agency structure that of administrator. Although these roles are not completely differentiated—a member of the clergy could serve as executive director of a state Catholic conference—the trend over time has been toward increasing differentiation. Already in 1970, only two executive directors were priests. For Sheehan, this signaled an early triumph of the spirit of Vatican II, which promoted a more active role for the laity in the church. In his words, "The State Conferences have achieved this lay involvement beautifully" (p. 48). Political scientist Mary Hanna has observed this on the national level: "Although the Catholic Church historically had been led almost entirely by clerics with seminary educations"— think of Fr. John Burke and Fr. John Ryan in the early days of the National Catholic Welfare Council—"the bishops, from the beginning in 1966, staffed the [United States Catholic Conference] with highly trained professionals, many of them with advanced degrees from the country's most prestigious secular universities."[15]

Sociologically, this dual structure can be seen as an organizational adaptation to an environment (state government) that was founded on rational-legal rather than traditional or charismatic authority. Hence, underlying the distinction between authority and agency structures is a crucial difference in bases of legitimate authority. According to Chaves, "The primary basis of legitimate authority within the religious authority structure is either *traditional* or *charismatic*. Pastors and bishops have legitimate religious authority to the extent that they either hold an office traditionally endowed with authority or possess a recognized claim to special insight into matters religious."

In the case of Roman Catholicism, the legitimacy of the religious authority structure rests on the tradition of apostolic succession. "Legitimate authority within the agency structure, by contrast, is *rational-legal*," Chaves continues. "The executive director of an agency is much like a division head in a corporation, with a great deal of authority over the work-related tasks of agency employees." And, as Max Weber argued in his explication of rational-legal authority structures (i.e., bureaucracies), holding an executive position in an organization "presupposes thorough training in a field of specialization."[16] Furthermore, unlike authority structures, the practices of agency structures properly conform to the institutional environment within which they operate. As we will see later in the book, these properties of religious agency structures are crucial to understanding the bishops' involvement in politics.

Authority Structure: Bishops as Board of Directors

The board of directors is the highest decision-making body in most state Catholic conferences. In some cases, this body is called the board of governors (Kansas, Massachusetts, Pennsylvania), in other cases the administrative board (New York) or board of trustees (Florida). In every case, these boards bear ultimate responsibility for the administration of conferences as corporations under civil law.[17] In her canonical analysis of the constitution and bylaws of the Massachusetts Catholic Conference, Marie Hilliard offers a description of its board of governors that adequately captures the reality in most states: "It controls all property, approves the annual budget, approves conference principles, determines policies, and makes official statements for the conference directly or through a designee."[18] Although their composition varies from state to state, the bishops dominate these boards, both *de jure* and *de facto*.

In 1970, Michael Sheehan found that almost 40 percent (7 of 18) of conferences restricted membership on the board of directors to bishops (p. 38). When he updated his research in 1975, 17 of 28 conferences (61 percent) had similar restrictions, including two (Illinois and Texas) that had mixed composition boards but restricted voting to the bishops.[19] By 2003, my research found that 22 of 32 conferences (69 percent) restricted board membership or voting to bishops (see table A.3 in appendix A). A clear trend toward exclusive episcopal control is apparent in these analyses, making plain the differentiation between authority and agency structures in the church.

The Connecticut Catholic Conference is instructive here. When it was established, the Connecticut Catholic Conference board included the ordinary and auxiliary bishops of the state (at the time there were five), as well as one priest and three lay (non-ordained) persons from each of the state's three dioceses. According to Sheehan, the non-ordained were represented initially by five men and four women (including two nuns) (p. 39). In her more recent analysis, Hilliard reports that in 1990 the executive director of the Connecticut Catholic Conference, William Wholean, was asked by his board of directors to study the organizational structure of other state conferences. Examining 21 conferences, he concluded that "there existed a vast variety of mechanisms to receive input from the laity, but most reserved decisions to the bishops."[20] When the Connecticut Conference revised its bylaws in 1992, non-bishops were removed from the board of directors. This same pattern of development can be seen also in Alaska, Kansas, Texas (which had always restricted voting to bishops), and Wisconsin. Since 1975, only the Washington State Catholic Conference has expanded its board beyond the bishops of the state, adding three representatives from each of the three dioceses, including at least one male and one female layperson from each diocese.

Even in those cases where state Catholic conferences have mixed composition boards—including both bishops and others—the ultimate authority rests with the bishops. In some cases, this is by law. With 42 total members, Illinois has by far the largest board of directors. It includes 6 ordinaries, 15 retired and auxiliary bishops, 5 priests, 5 religious, and 11 lay members. However, only the 6 ordinaries are *voting* members. The other 36 members serve an advisory role. Similarly, the Iowa Catholic Conference has 27 members on its diverse board, but only the 6 active and retired bishops of Iowa are voting members.

In other cases, the bishops' dominance of the board of directors is not by law but in fact. One conference director with a mixed composition board explains, "They're equal, but they're not really equal. It's never said, 'But you don't really have a vote on the board'—where it is lay people against the bishops. You just don't have it that way. I can tell you of instances when a lay person with a good voice would express his or her concern [about an issue] and the bishops listen to it, but it would still pass."

Moreover, in those states with a *cardinal* archbishop—California
(Los Angeles); Illinois (Chicago); Maryland (Baltimore and Washington, D.C.); Massachusetts (Boston, until 2002); Michigan (Detroit);
New York (New York); and Pennsylvania (Philadelphia)—the board
dynamics may differ as well. The case of Cardinal Adam Maida of Detroit is instructive. According to Paul Long, vice president for public
policy of the Michigan Catholic Conference, "By virtue of our by-laws
and constitution the Cardinal Archbishop of Detroit is the Chairman
of the Board of Directors. The Cardinal is a strong leader and sets the
tone to ensure the mission and purpose of the Conference is faithfully
reflected in its activities. I think in our case, with this chairman, his
position, experience and leadership provide a strong influence on the
deliberations of our Board."

In their analyses, both Sheehan and Hilliard highlight the benefits
of having non-bishops on a board of directors. Sheehan speaks ap-
provingly of boards being "representative of the various aspects of the
Church" (p. 39). Hilliard argues that "inclusion of laity on the board
would provide consistency with conciliar teaching" on the importance of lay participation in the saving mission of the church (*Lumen
Gentium*, no. 33) and "assure the conference of experts in the various
issues of public policy."[21] In many conferences, laypeople—as well as
priests and religious—do play a consultative role, whether or not they
are not represented on the board of directors. The administrative
board of the Maryland Catholic Conference (described in chapter 1)
is an excellent example of this. Having a wider membership than just
the bishops allows for richer and fuller deliberations on issues, to be
sure. But only bishops, whether *de jure* or *de facto*, have decision-
making power in most state Catholic conferences. They are at the
center of the church's authority structure.

Agency Structure: Professional Staff as Secretariat

In understanding the agency structure of state Catholic conferences—
the professional staff or secretariat that run the conferences on a day-to-
day basis—it is important to focus on the position of executive director.
Executive directors are key to the successful operation of the conferences. As Sheehan wrote in 1970,

> He, more than anyone, is responsible for the success or failure of the
> Conference. He is the one whom the board of directors relies on to

carry out the policy set by the board on a day-to-day basis. He usually has full responsibility for carrying out the Conference objectives and programs. He submits budgets, prepares the agendas for the meetings, arranges committee appointments and work. He does lobbying, either formally or informally with the state government, coordinates the opinions of the bishops and diocesan officials, gives talks throughout the state on the work of the Conference. (p. 31)

As conference staffs have grown over the years, some executive directors are able to delegate a portion of these responsibilities to others. Still, the core point of Sheehan's description remains true to this day: the position and person of the executive director is at the heart of the work of state Catholic conferences as agency structures.

To be sure, the 30 years since Sheehan wrote have brought some important changes. Sheehan's use of the masculine pronoun ("he") in his description of executive directors was appropriate to 1970, when all 22 conference directors were men. But as of December 2004, 4 of 34 conferences (12 percent) were headed by women: Connecticut (Dr. Marie Hilliard); Iowa (Sara Eide); Michigan (Sr. Monica Kostielney, R.S.M.), and Washington (Sr. Sharon Park, O.P.).[22] Moreover, none of the conference directors listed in Sheehan's dissertation still heads a conference. Two of the longest-standing directors, Kirby Ducote of Louisiana and Cheatham Hodges of Georgia, bade farewell at the fall 2001 meeting of the National Association of State Catholic Conference Directors. The following year, 18-year veteran Msgr. Edward Ryle of Arizona and 12-year veteran Jane Chiles of Kentucky also retired.

Even with these retirements, state Catholic conference executive directors as a group remain very experienced. At the end of 2002, the average number of years as director of the same conference was nearly a decade (9.25 years), and the average number of years on the same conference staff was even higher (12.63 years), as several directors have been promoted from within their own conference. Currently, the most senior conference director is Gerald D'Avolio, who has directed the Massachusetts Catholic Conference for 28 years. Richard Daly has been on the staff of the Texas Catholic Conference for 30 years, 25 of them as its executive director. The directors in Florida (Dr. D. Michael McCarron), Maryland (Dick Dowling), Michigan (Sr. Monica), Nebraska (James Cunningham), New Jersey (William Bolan), Ohio (Timothy Luckhaupt), Oregon (Robert

Castagna), and Washington (Sr. Sharon) all have 20 or more years of experience with their conferences.

Another key area of change concerns the professional background of conference directors. Here we see two seemingly contradictory movements. On the one hand, more directors are ordained or vowed religious today than in 1970; on the other hand, government (and especially legislative) experience is becoming more important. Some further investigation helps to reconcile these two developments. In 1970, Sheehan observed that "the executive director is usually a layman" (p. 31). At the time, only 2 of 22 conferences, Illinois and New Jersey, were headed by priests (and none were led by religious). Since then, both conferences have made the lay movement, New Jersey in 1972 and Illinois in 1986. Surprisingly, however, by 2003, 6 of 34 conferences were headed by individuals who were either ordained or vowed religious. The Catholic conference in West Virginia is headed by a priest, Rev. John Gallagher, V.G.; Michigan and Washington are headed by religious sisters, Sr. Monica and Sr. Sharon; Texas by a religious brother, Bro. Richard; and Missouri and Hawaii by permanent deacons, Rev. Mr. Lawrence Weber and Rev. Mr. Walter Yoshimitsu.[23] Thus, the proportion of conferences headed by individuals who are ordained or vowed religious nearly doubled, from 9 percent to 17.6 percent, between 1970 and 2003.

These six cases, however, require a closer look to fully understand the dynamics of state Catholic conferences as agency structures. Although the Michigan Catholic Conference is headed by Sr. Monica, it also employs a layman, Mr. Paul Long, as its vice president for public policy. Similarly, Sr. Sharon heads the Catholic conference in Washington State, but also employs a separate contract lobbyist. And Deacon Larry, who heads the Missouri Catholic Conference, has a law degree and extensive legislative and governmental experience that preceded his ordination into the permanent diaconate. Clearly, the vast majority of conferences (if not all of them) recognize that political advocacy is a specialized activity, and not necessarily one for which the primary qualification is theological training. An advertisement in 2002 for the position of executive director of the Colorado Catholic Conference exemplifies this:

> The position advises Colorado's five Catholic Bishops on issues of public policy and acts as the professional lobbyist for the Archdiocese of Denver, the Diocese of Pueblo and the Diocese of Colorado Springs.

Requires Bachelor's degree, a J.D. or graduate degree in public policy preferred. Experience as a lobbyist, or equivalent legislative, executive, administrative or public policy experience required. Strong knowledge of Catholic social teaching and the ability to develop rapport with legislators, lobbyists and other organizations required. Must be a Roman Catholic in good standing with the Church.

In this advertisement, Colorado is following in the footsteps of other state conferences that have hired executive directors recently. Ronald Johnson was hired in 2003 as executive director of the Arizona Catholic Conference after working as the director of government relations for the State Bar of Arizona. Sara Eide joined the Iowa Catholic Conference in 2000 and was promoted to executive director in 2003 after having served for three years as an aide to the majority leader of the Iowa State Senate. Vincent Senior took over the Catholic Conference of Kentucky in 2002 after a long career with Reynolds Metals Company, including managing its state and local government relations across the United States. Michael Farmer was a veteran state legislator, in line to become speaker of the Kansas House of Representatives, when the bishops of Kansas hired him to serve as executive director of their conference.

Already in 1970, the predominant professional background of executive directors was law (see table 2.6), followed by business and management. These two backgrounds together accounted for over two-thirds of all conference directors at the time.

Table 2.6. Professional Background of State Catholic Conference Executive Directors, 1970 and 2002

Professional Background	1970	2002
Law	43%	28.5%
Business and Management	26	7
Military	10.5	0
Public Relations	10.5	3.5
Legislative	5	25
Church Administration	5	11
Education	—	14.5
Government Administration	—	7
Community Service	—	3.5

Notes: The categories and 19 responses for 1970 are from Sheehan, *The State Catholic Conference*, p. 31. Data from 2002 are from my State Catholic Conference Survey 2002.

By 2002, the backgrounds of executive directors had become both more diverse and in some respects more standardized. Law remains the most common professional background, but it has lost market share over the decades. Business and management have lost even more, dropping from second to fifth most common. The big winner since 1970 has been legislative experience, whose gain mirrored management's loss, rising from fifth to second. Combining legislative experience with government administration, we find work in state government (whether legislative or administrative) is now the principal professional background of one-third of executive directors. It also should be noted that nearly one-third (32.1 percent) of executive directors were promoted from within their own conferences, giving them valuable legislative experience regardless of their professional background.

Not surprisingly, given the actual background of executive directors in 1970, Sheehan reports that respondents to his survey "almost unanimously said that the ideal background for the job of executive director of a State Conference was either law or management" (p. 31).[24] In my 2002 survey, I replicated Sheehan's question and found some significant change in the ranking of important backgrounds. The near unanimous agreement on the importance of law and management in 1970 has given way to a different ranking and more diversity of opinion in 2002.

As table 2.7 shows, law and management have been superceded by legislative experience as the most important background for an executive director. Indeed, legislative experience is now the clear top choice; to wit: the average ranking (1.66) is less than half that of management, the second most highly ranked background (3.53).

Table 2.7.   Ranking of Most Important Backgrounds for Executive Directors, 2002

Background	Overall Rank	Average Ranking	Range of Ranking
Legislative Experience	1	1.66	1 to 5
Management	2	3.53	1 to 6
Public Relations	3	3.59	1 to 7
Law	4	3.66	1 to 8
Theological Training	5	4.09	1 to 8
Teaching	6	5.66	3 to 8
Business	7	6.31	3 to 8
Sales	8	7.50	4 to 8

Although five different backgrounds were ranked number one by at least one respondent, over half of the respondents (56.3 percent) ranked legislative experience as their top choice. The background with the next highest number of number-one rankings is actually theological training (15.6 percent). The fact that the overall rank of theological training is fifth out of eight possible positions suggests that the collective opinion of respondents is fairly polarized about the value of theological training.[25] In second place, management narrowly beats out public relations, which is closely followed by law. This suggests that perceptions have not been totally revolutionized. Still, the rise of legislative experience to the top suggests an important change in how current executive directors see their roles compared to executive directors 30 years ago. Conference leadership continues to adapt to the exigencies of its organizational environment.

Together, tables 2.6 and 2.7 strongly support the conclusion that, in both actual and desirable professional background, legislative experience is becoming the dominant trait of the state Catholic conference director. But focusing exclusively on this element only tells part of the story. Collectively, conference directors are a very accomplished group of individuals regardless of their professional backgrounds. Over half (57.1 percent) hold doctorates (J.D. or Ph.D.), and many came to head conferences after distinguished careers in other areas. For example, Dr. Marie Hilliard, executive director of the Connecticut Catholic Conference, is a registered nurse and medical ethicist who has served as the executive officer of the Connecticut Board of Examiners for Nursing and as a member of the Board of Directors of the National Council of State Boards of Nursing. She is also a lieutenant colonel in the United States Army Reserve and has recently completed a licentiate in canon law at the Catholic University of America. Dr. Thomas Feld joined the Iowa Catholic Conference in 1999 after serving as president of Mount Mercy College in Cedar Rapids for 22 years, where he is now president emeritus. V. Robert Payant of Nevada is a retired judge for Michigan's 41st Circuit Court and former president of the National Judicial College. And so on.

Relationship between Authority and Agency Structures in Practice

Although state Catholic conferences are best characterized as dual structures, there are times when bishops do get directly involved in political advocacy. Archbishop Weakland's letter on welfare reform in the *Washington Post* which opened this book is a notable example, as is Cardinal McCarrick's defense of the seal of confession that was discussed in chapter 1. In 2000, Cardinal Anthony Bevilacqua of Philadelphia was brought to the legislature to testify in favor of a moratorium on the death penalty. According to Pennsylvania Catholic Conference director Robert O'Hara, "It was somewhat historic. I don't think a cardinal's ever done that before in Pennsylvania. And I wouldn't have prevailed upon him, but he was immediately willing." At the same time, O'Hara comments, "In most cases, we do not shoot the cannon if we don't have to. In this situation the cardinal was very interested in presenting the church's position on the death penalty."

For the most part, though, the staff of the conferences do not prevail on the bishops. In turn, the bishops leave the day-to-day political activities of the conferences to the professionals they have hired, in no small part because they hire such competent and trustworthy individuals as staff. As Dick Dowling of Maryland puts it, "If trust manifests itself in freedom, trust is very high." Says Paul Long of the Michigan Catholic Conference, "Our bishops express interest by their deliberation and support. Policy is formulated at Board meetings based on staff research. Implementation of any Board action is carried out by staff. They say, 'You know, that is why we have you.'"

Although conference directors are given autonomy to do their work, they are very careful not to act without regard to the bishops. In fact, their overarching goal is to faithfully represent the bishops' views and priorities. Some of this is due to the legal background of many directors. For example, William Bolan of New Jersey describes the bishops as his "clients" to whom he (presumably) has a fiduciary obligation to represent their interests and desires, not his. Francis Clinch, who served briefly as the executive director of the Montana Catholic Conference in 2003 and 2004, also brought a lawyer's mentality to the job. "An attorney should represent his client, and do it zealously," he told the *Montana Catholic* newspaper. "My job here is to make the voice and position of the bishops clearly felt and understood."[26] Mostly, though, it is out of respect for the authority of the office of bishop. Upon his retirement as the founding executive director of the Georgia Catholic Conference, Cheatham Hodges recalled the instruction Archbishop Thomas Donnellan of Atlanta gave him upon his appointment: "Remember—you are us—the bishop of Savannah and the bishop of Atlanta." According to an article in the *Georgia Bulletin,* he never forgot.[27]

Like his peers, Robert O'Hara maintains regular contact with his bishops, especially Nicholas Datillo, the bishop of Harrisburg who is the president of the Pennsylvania Catholic Conference, and, when necessary, Cardinal Anthony Bevilacqua (until 2003 the archbishop of Philadelphia). When we spoke early in 2002, O'Hara told me, "As a matter of fact, right now I have a call in to Cardinal Bevilacqua. It's a minor matter, but I talked to Bishop Dattilo about it. I said to him that even though it's a minor matter I'd like to run it by the cardinal just so he's aware. I wanted to extend him the courtesy of making sure that he knows about this, so that he doesn't hear about it from somebody else. Bishop Dattilo was 100 percent in agreement with what I thought. He didn't think that it was anything that required an OK from the cardinal, but agreed with me that it would be nice to make sure that he knows about it." Many of the issues the conferences deal with are "no-brainers" in terms of formulating an official church position, and so conference staff are given latitude to address those issues using their best judgment as professionals. Still, conference staffs tend to proceed cautiously, earning their autonomy through fidelity to their bishops.

Conference Staff as Lay Apostolate

To characterize those executive directors who directly engage the public policy process as "lobbyists" could be seen as an insult given popular perceptions of that breed of political influence peddlers. But if lobbyists are those who "deliberate[ly] attempt to influence political decisions through various forms of public advocacy," then most fit the description (and those who do not, hire others to lobby for them). Directors are lobbyists, then, but not in the basest sense of the term. One reason people dislike lobbyists is that they are seen as "hired guns"—willing to represent any client on any issue as long as they get paid. As one lobbyist commented in a book on the ethics of lobbying, "the lobbyist is simply a hired gun. Lobbyists have no principles. Lobbyists have no positions. You ask someone what do you think about this and he'll say I don't know, I don't have a client. We're sort of agnostics here. A client retains us and that's fine, but if someone who didn't like that client retained us, well, that would be fine too."[28]

Conference staff who represent the church in the legislative arena are emphatically not hired guns. Most are accomplished professionals who had or have other work options and choose to serve the church in this way. Indeed, perhaps the best way to understand working for a state Catholic conference is as participation in the "lay apostolate."

The idea of a lay apostolate has deep roots in the Catholic tradition, stretching back at least to the Apostolic Age and the Epistle to Diognetus, which declares, "Christians must be to the world what the soul is to the body."[29] This idea was strongly reemphasized at the Second Vatican Council, particularly in the "Dogmatic Constitution on the Church" (*Lumen Gentium*), which quotes this early church epistle. Whereas clergy and bishops are called to ministry in the church, the laity are called to act as apostles in the world. According to *Lumen Gentium*,

> What specifically characterizes the laity is their secular nature. . . . The laity, by their very vocation, seek the kingdom of God by engaging in temporal affairs and by ordering them according to the plan of God. They live in the world, that is, in each and in all of the secular professions and occupations. They live in the ordinary circumstances of family and social life, from which the very web of their existence is woven. They are called there by God that by exercising their proper function and led by the spirit of the Gospel, they may work for the sanctification of the world from within as a leaven. (no. 31)

These ideas are reiterated and elaborated in the Council's "Decree on the Apostolate of the Laity" (*Apostolicam Actuositatem*) and again in the *Catechism of the Catholic Church* (no. 899).

Although the staff I interviewed never used the term "lay apostolate," it is clear from the way they spoke about their work that they are living out this vocational call in their conference work. Consider the case of Sara Eide, executive director of the Iowa Catholic Conference since 2003. After graduating from the University of Iowa in 1995, she spent two years working at a Jesuit mission in Ecuador. When she returned to Iowa she took a job working for the majority leader of the Iowa State Senate. Three years later, she was looking for a change and applied to work for Catholic Relief Services (CRS). Eide recalls the events that followed:

> I flew out to Baltimore, interviewed for a position with CRS out there, and came back. The next day, Tom Feld, the executive director of the

Iowa Catholic Conference at the time, stopped into the majority leader's office and wanted to visit about an issue. So we got to talking, and I asked him if I could use him as a reference if Catholic Relief Services called for references. He said, "So, you're interested in a different job?" I said, "Yeah, I'm ready for a change." And he said, "Well what about working for the Iowa Catholic Conference?" I said, "I'd love to." He said, "Give me 24 hours." He called me the next morning and said, "Can you come down to our office and visit about this?" So I went down, and he had already talked to the archbishop and had gotten his blessing. We talked and he offered me the job that day. And I really wasn't sure where I was going at that time in my life. I was praying about what God wanted me to do, and so it was pretty clear that this is where He wanted me to go.

Robert Castagna also felt called to his work at the Oregon Catholic Conference, as he states succinctly: "For me it's a perfect blend of my faith, my interest in theology, my training as a lawyer, and my interest in public policy. To me it was the natural evolution of my life's interest, course, and vocation."

Thus, although it is true that conference staff are increasingly drawn from the state government arena, it is equally true that these political insiders are deeply dedicated to the faith and the church. After 20-plus years as executive director of the Massachusetts Catholic Conference, Gerald D'Avolio maintains that the attribute that has been most important to him in his job is "total commitment to the Catholic Church and its great and wonderful teachings." He adds, "When I look at potential staff, my first inquiry and my assessment of the individual is total and unwavering belief and support for the Catholic Church and its teaching. That is my number one priority."

I cannot claim it is a common practice, but my experience at the Florida Catholic Conference in the spring of 2003 demonstrated the centrality of faith to their work. The Florida conference occupies the entire first floor and part of a second floor of offices in a small office building annex about two blocks from the Florida statehouse. Their complex consists of nine offices and three cubicles for their 12 staff, plus the Horkan-Gallagher conference room—named after the founding executive director, Thomas Horkan, and their first associate for social concerns, Rosemary Flahive Gallagher. At the center of the conference room is a three-sided (Trinitarian) table that was crafted by the current executive director, D. Michael McCarron, and his neighbor. As a centerpiece, a lectionary lays opened to the day's Mass

readings on top of a carved stand. Alongside sits a gold crucifix and a
votive candle. (During my visit, there was also a small card with a
"prayer for peace" on it, in recognition that the United States was on
the brink of waging war on Saddam Hussein's regime in Iraq.) This is
the setting for the prayer and Word service that the conference staff
holds most afternoons. Despite the fact that the legislative session was
in full swing during my visit, these daily services were attended by
two-thirds of the staff. A rosary is also prayed in this room on most
Wednesday mornings and on Fridays during the season of Lent.

CONCLUSION

This chapter addresses state Catholic conferences from an organizational perspective. It shows that, already in their founding, the dual
structure of state Catholic conferences was well adapted to America's
secular political system. Furthermore, as they have grown and ma-
tured over the years, the professionalization of the lay secretariat
(the agency structure) has made them even more so. At the same
time, the conferences remain firmly rooted in the authority structure
of the church. The differentiation of the authority structure from the
agency structure does not necessarily lead to the secularization of the
agency structure seen in many denominational agencies. The fact that
the secretariat remains closely tethered to the bishops organizationally and committed to representing the bishops personally prevents
this internal secularization from taking place. In the end, having one
foot planted in the church and one in the political arena, state
Catholic conferences are well suited to being faithful *and* effective
representatives of the church in state politics. The following three
chapters document this with respect to the issues, legitimacy, and discourse of the conferences in statehouses across the country.

NOTES

1. Rev. Michael J. Sheehan, *The State Catholic Conference: A New Development in Interecclesial Cooperation in the United States*, (excerpt from a
dissertation presented for the degree of Doctor of Canon Law, Pontifical Lateran University, Rome, 1971). Citations to Sheehan's dissertation in the present book refer to this 114-page excerpt of the original dissertation which

includes a brief introduction, chapter 3, and the conclusion. The document is available in the papers of Thomas J. Gumbleton, auxiliary bishop of Detroit, at the University of Notre Dame Archives, Notre Dame, IN 46556 (CGUM 02/02). In 1971, Sheehan was a priest of the Diocese of Dallas. He has since been elevated to archbishop of Santa Fe, New Mexico.

2. *A note on measures of central tendency*: In the presentation of the summary statistics in this chapter, unless otherwise specified, "average" refers to the *mean* value. Also known as the "arithmetic average," the mean is the sum of the individual values divided by the number of cases. When appropriate, the *median* value is also given. The median is the value above and below which half the cases fall (i.e., the 50th percentile). Unlike the mean, which can be skewed by a few extremely high or low values, the median is a measure of central tendency not sensitive to "outliers" (e.g., the "average" income in the United States almost always refers to the median income to control for the billionaires who otherwise skew the mean income).

3. In *The State Catholic Conference*, Sheehan observes that "although some of the Conferences predated the Second Vatican Council even those Conferences have been heavily influenced by the Council and most have been reorganized in order to put into effect the Council teachings" (pp. 21–22). Given the close connection between conferences and the Council, is important to recall that the Council's "Decree on Bishops" (*Christus Dominus*) and the related canons of the 1983 Code of Canon Law speak explicitly only about national and regional episcopal conferences (such as the United State Conference of Catholic Bishops). Although analogous to national conferences in many ways, state-level episcopal conferences are *non-canonical* entities and so are limited in their power to create and enforce church policies.

In the same way the National Catholic Welfare Council was forced to substitute "*Conference*" for "Council" so as not to be confused with general councils (see chapter 1), it would probably be best if state Catholic conferences were not called "conferences" so the distinction between canonical and non-canonical entities would be reinforced. The fact that they perform some analogous functions to the national episcopal conference seems to outweigh this technical concern. The recent consolidation of the canonical National Conference of Catholic Bishops (NCCB) and non-canonical United States Catholic Conference (USCC) into a single entity, the United States Conference of Catholic Bishops (USCCB), internalizes the distinction between the canonical and non-canonical dimensions and, to my mind, only confuses matters more.

In 1970, Sheehan noted that "the State Catholic Conference could become a moral person [i.e., a canonical juridic being in the church] by the special concession of a competent superior. This has not happened and probably never will. The bishops prefer to keep the State Conferences less formal, voluntary and amicable gatherings with practical and pastoral ends" (p. 41).

Given decreasing support among some American bishops for episcopal conferences (which I discuss in the concluding chapter), it is probably even less likely today than it was when Sheehan was writing.

4. Some of this description of Virginia is derived from a conversation with Rev. Gerald Fogarty, S.J., Kenan Professor of Church History at the University of Virginia, and his recent book *Commonwealth Catholicism: A History of the Catholic Church in Virginia* (Notre Dame, IN: University of Notre Dame Press, 2001), chapter 28.

5. As I was completing this book, the bishops of Virginia announced that they were forming a Catholic Conference to represent its interests in Richmond.

6. The hyperbole here ought not obscure the kernel of truth in this comment. West is clearly speaking of church-state separation more in political terms than legal terms. Patty Henetz, "Catholic Church a Player in Rhode Island Government," Associated Press wire story, 17 May 2003.

7. These statistics on staff size and budgets do not include the Michigan Catholic Conference, which is unique among state conferences in that it administers employee benefits programs for church employees (clergy and laity) and property-casualty loss fund programs for the church throughout and beyond Michigan. This business side of the conference's operation considerably increases both its staff and budget. To wit, the Michigan Catholic Conference has about 45 employees, of which only 4 work in the public policy division. The Michigan conference's material abundance is best exemplified by its new $13 million, four-story, 50,000-square-foot office complex in Lansing that was dedicated in 2003 (see "Neighbors Glad to See Upgrade to South End of Downtown: New Catholic Conference Building Open," *Lansing State Journal*, 13 March 2003).

8. Marie Hilliard, *State Catholic Conferences: A Canonical Analysis of Two Constitutions and Bylaws* (Licentiate in Canon Law thesis, The Catholic University of America, Washington, DC, 2003), pp. 11, 33.

9. Reese, *A Flock of Shepherds*, p. 19.

10. Hilliard, *State Catholic Conferences*, pp. 4, 7.

11. Hilliard, *State Catholic Conferences*, p. 33.

12. The executive director of the other conference declined to be identified.

13. Mark Chaves, "Intraorganizational Power and Internal Secularization in Protestant Denominations," *American Journal of Sociology* 99 (1993): 8.

14. Mark Chaves, "Denominations as Dual Structures: An Organizational Analysis," *Sociology of Religion* 54 (1993): 155.

15. Mary Hanna, "Bishops as Political Leaders," pp. 75–86 in Charles Dunn, ed., *Religion in American Politics* (Washington, DC: Congressional Quarterly Press, 1989), p. 78.

16. Chaves, "Denominations as Dual Structures," p. 157; Max Weber, *Economy and Society: An Outline of Interpretive Sociology*, ed. Claus Wittich and Guenther Roth (Berkeley: University of California Press, 1979), p. 958.

17. Sheehan, *The State Catholic Conference*, p. 36.

18. Hilliard, *State Catholic Conferences*, p. 35. As Sheehan describes it, "The board of directors of the State Conferences sets the policy for the Conference, indicates the priorities, approves the budget and chooses the executive director. The members of the board review the work of the Conference and confer regularly with one another and the director to ensure the success of the Conference" (*The State Catholic Conference*, p. 36).

19. Michael Sheehan, "State Catholic Conferences," *The Jurist* 35 (1975): 431–54, table 4.

20. Hilliard, *State Catholic Conferences*, p. 25.

21. Hilliard, *State Catholic Conferences*, p. 46.

22. It could have been as high as 6 of 34, but the executive director of the Catholic Conference of Kentucky, Mrs. Jane Chiles, retired for health reasons in July 2002 and was replaced by Mr. Vincent Senior, and the executive director of the Montana Catholic Conference, Ms. Lani Kobelia Candelora, was replaced by Mr. Francis Clinch in the fall of 2003.

23. Mr. Ronald Johnson (a layman) replaced Monsignor Edward Ryle as executive director of the Arizona Catholic Conference early in 2003.

24. Sheehan's data are reported on p. 31 and drawn from question 10 of his survey (reprinted as appendix 2 of *The State Catholic Conference*, pp. 92–94).

25. In technical terms, the standard deviation of the ranking of theological training (2.107) was 40 percent higher than the average standard deviation for the eight categories being ranked (1.505).

26. Quoted in Eric Schiedermayer, "New MCC Executive Director Prepares to Represent Montana Bishops," *The Montana Catholic Online*, January 2004, http://www.diocesehelena.org/mtcath/jan04/mcc.htm (accessed 1 March 2004).

27. Gretchen Keiser, "Cheatham Hodges Retires as Georgia's First Catholic Conference Representative," *Georgia Bulletin*, 4 July 2002.

28. Woodstock Theological Center, *The Ethics of Lobbying: Organized Interests, Political Power, and the Common Good* (Washington, DC: Georgetown University Press, 2002), pp. 24, 7–8.

29. Russell Shaw, *Ministry or Apostolate? What Should the Catholic Laity Be Doing?* (Huntington, IN: Our Sunday Visitor, 2002), pp. 44–45.

3

Issues

The Seamless Garment in Action

For over a decade, John Carr has served as the director of the United States Conference of Catholic Bishops' Department of Social Development and World Peace. One day, returning from work in Washington, D.C., he stopped at a grocery store. After shopping, he approached the cash register, still wearing the identification card around his neck that gives his office and title. Seeing this, the checker grabbed his name card and asked, "Do you work for the Catholic bishops?"

"Yes."

"Are you in charge of world peace?"

"Sort of," Carr responded with a laugh.

"Well, you need to do a better job!"

Carr's brief and humorous story highlights the seeming absurdity of having a department for "social development" *and* "world peace"— as if each alone were not an overwhelming responsibility. But, in fact, among the Catholic Church's public concerns is the promotion of world peace and social development. The church is not unique in bringing religious ideas and ideals into the public square, but Catholic theology creates a uniquely broad range of issues for engagement.

Recalling theologian Jaroslav Pelikan's distinction between traditionalism as "the dead faith of the living" and tradition as "the living faith of the dead,"[1] we can see "Catholic Social Teaching" as a tradition of thinking about the social world from a Catholic perspective. This tradition has its origins in Jesus Christ's ministry and teaching, from the Beatitudes ("Blessed are the . . .") and the Great Commandment

("'Love the Lord your God . . .' and 'Love your neighbor as yourself'")
to his hard teachings on poverty and wealth (the parables of the rich
man and Lazarus and the rich young man).[2] In its modern incarnation,
from Leo XIII and Pius XI to Pius XII and John XXIII, the social teaching of the church became more open to democracy and more positive
about the world overall.[3] These developments were codified and
given an ecumenical endorsement by the bishops worldwide gathered
at the Second Vatican Council when they promulgated *Gaudium et
Spes* ("Pastoral Constitution on the Church in the Modern World"). This
document linked together for the first time the various themes in the
social teaching of the church and tied them clearly to a particular
Christian theological anthropology centered on the nature of human
freedom and dignity and the good society in which those human po-
tentialities could be fulfilled. Through his prolific writing, Pope John
Paul II has continued to develop Catholic Social Teaching, anchoring
it in the need to protect "the dignity of the human person," a phrase
that appears repeatedly in his writing and speeches.[4]

The complex, living tradition of Catholic Social Teaching now consists of hundreds of pages of primary texts and thousands of pages of
interpretation and commentary. It is too much even for most educated
Catholics to assimilate. Fortunately, the tradition was usefully summarized by Chicago archbishop Joseph Cardinal Bernardin in his 1983
Gannon Lecture at Fordham University. Bernardin spoke of "a consistent ethic of life," the central idea of which is "the sacredness of human life and the responsibility we have, personally and socially, to
protect and preserve the sanctity of life." For Bernardin, this ethic was
comprehensive and consistent "from womb to tomb. . . . For the spectrum of life cuts across the issues of genetics, abortion, capital punishment, modern warfare and the care of the terminally ill."[5] He later
wrote, "We are convinced that we cannot have a just and compassionate society unless our care extends to both sides of the line of
birth: We must protect the basic right to life and, at the same time, promote the associated rights of nutrition, housing, and health care which
enhance the lives we have saved."[6] All of these various issues are wo-
ven together in Catholic Social Teaching into a *seamless garment*.[7]

The longstanding demand for social justice embodied in Catholic
Social Teaching, the positive view of church involvement in the world
offered by the Second Vatican Council, and Bernardin's call for a consistent ethic of life are the key ideological springboards for the politi-

cal advocacy of contemporary state Catholic conferences. It is the responsibility of the agency structure of the conferences to take these teachings and put them into action in the public policy arena.

AGENDAS, ISSUE HIERARCHIES, AND PRUDENTIAL JUDGMENTS

One of the first steps state Catholic conferences take in moving from theology to public policy is to articulate a legislative agenda. Perusing the legislative agendas of state Catholic conferences highlights just how encompassing the seamless garment is. Consider, for example, the typically middle-American state of Missouri. The 2004 public policy agenda of the Missouri Catholic Conference gives positions on over 40 issues, organized into nine broad areas:

1. *Respecting the sanctity of human life.* E.g., "The death penalty should be abolished" and "Abortions should be prohibited."
2. *Meeting basic human needs.* E.g., "The state and federal minimum wage should reflect the actual cost of living for individuals supporting themselves or their families."
3. *Adequate and accessible heath care.* E.g., "Funding and coverage for adult and children's Medicaid programs should be maintained" and "Pharmaceutical assistance programs should target those most in need."
4. *Welcoming the immigrant and refugee.* E.g., "Regardless of citizenship or immigration status, all persons have the right to basic essentials such as food, clothing, shelter and basic education."
5. *Sustainable rural and urban communities.* E.g., "Diversified and sustainable family farms should be promoted" and "Land and transportation policies should protect farmland while encouraging urban revitalization."
6. *Investing in a quality education for all.* E.g., "Parents have a fundamental right to select schools that meet the needs of their children and that are in accord with their religious convictions."
7. *Offenders, victims, and the community.* E.g., "Sentencing and inmate release policies should reflect restorative justice principles" and "A corrections ombudsman should be established to ensure humane prison policies and practices."

8. *Strengthening the family.* E.g., "State law should continue to define marriage as being between a man and a woman" and "The state should strengthen its response to domestic violence."
9. *Providing for the common good.* E.g., "The response to the current state budget crisis should provide priority attention to those most vulnerable" and "Predatory lending practices should be prohibited."

Such a broad, some might say unwieldy, agenda has led some to wonder whether state Catholic conferences would benefit from a more focused agenda.

Robert O'Hara from the Pennsylvania Catholic Conference recalls a conversation with a new member of his administrative board, a layperson who had been appointed by one of the state's bishops because of his experience working in public policy. According to O'Hara, "He understood the political process. He had actually worked on the staff of one of the senators at one time." At the first administrative board meeting of the legislative session, O'Hara distributed a list of the Pennsylvania Catholic Conference's public policy issues and priorities. Upon receiving the list of more than 30 public policy priorities, the new member said, "You know, you've got to cut these back. How in the world are you going to deal with this many issues? You have to get these down to six or seven main issues that you're working on and paying attention to." O'Hara responded, "All right. Can you tell me which issues you think we could drop or pay less attention to?" As they went through and discussed the various priorities, O'Hara prodded the board member, "How about this here? Is this something we can ignore if it comes up? Or do you think we shouldn't be pushing for this over here?" In the end, none of the priorities was stricken from the list. In fact, since that meeting, the number of issues on the Pennsylvania Catholic Conference's public policy agenda has increased from over 30 to over 40.

O'Hara's inclusiveness notwithstanding, not every priority on a state Catholic conference agenda has equal weight. There have always been some bishops who see abortion as the fundamental political issue, from Cardinals John Krol of Philadelphia and John Cody of Chicago in the 1970s to Cardinals Bernard Law of Boston and John O'Connor of New York in the 1980s and 1990s to Archbishops John Myers of Newark and Raymond Burke of St. Louis today. Many are skeptical of the suggestion that there is an equivalence between abortion and other issues like nuclear war or welfare or capital punishment. But one can see a connection between these various issues without claiming that they are all equivalent. As Cardinal Bernardin himself said, "Surely we can all agree that the taking of human life in abortion is not the same as failing to protect human dignity against hunger. But having made that distinction, let us not fail to make the point that both are moral issues requiring a response of the Catholic community and of our society as a whole." Similarly, in the 2001 "Pastoral Plan for Pro-Life Activities," the United States Conference of Catholic Bishops maintained, "A consistent ethic of life, which explains the Church's teaching at the level of moral principle—far from diminishing concern for abortion and euthanasia or equating all issues touching on the dignity of human life—recognizes instead the distinctive character of each issue while giving each its proper place within a coherent moral vision."[8]

These clarifications notwithstanding, some more orthodox Catholics, like theologian George Wiegel, see the seamless garment as "tattered." As Wiegel told the *National Catholic Reporter* in the wake of the 2004 U.S. presidential election, "We now know, because [John] Kerry has demonstrated it, that the seamless garment metaphor, whatever truths it embodies within it, becomes in the hands of politicians an excuse [to oppose church teaching on life issues]. Why are we trying to stitch the thing together again?"[9] But this is a criticism not of the seamless garment metaphor itself, but of the use to which it is put. Although some left-leaning Catholics surely use it to downplay "pelvic issues" (abortion, cloning, euthanasia) and play up "social justice" issues (poverty, war), seeing all of these issues as being connected along a spectrum of life—"from womb to tomb"—does not require this. In fact, state Catholic conferences advocate a consistent life ethic without seeing all the various threads in the seamless garment as equally prominent.

Asked to list the top 5 specific policy issues on which they work in order of priority, 31 conference directors collectively named 20 different issues. These issues included Indian affairs, the environment, immigrants, religious freedom, and urban development. But among these 20 issues, a distinct hierarchy clearly emerges. To construct a ranking, I assigned an issue five points for being named by a conference director as the highest-priority issue, four points for being

Table 3.1.   Hierarchy of Policy Issues

Issue Domain	Total Ranking Points
Pro-Life	120
Education	107
Economic Justice	78
Health Care	38
Criminal Justice	28

named as second highest, and so on. This procedure yields the rank order depicted in table 3.1, with the total points earned demonstrating the magnitude of difference between the issues.

Pro-life concerns clearly are the highest-priority issue for state Catholic conferences collectively.[10] Of 31 conference directors surveyed, 20 named pro-life issues as the top priority for their conference. Education issues follow closely on the heels of pro-life concerns, mainly on the strength of being named most commonly as the second and third highest-priority issue for state Catholic conferences. These two issues are historically the bread-and-butter issues of the Catholic Church in state legislative politics. There is a considerable drop-off from the top two to the third, fourth, and fifth highest-priority issues for state Catholic conferences. Economic justice, health care, and criminal justice all fit squarely within the boundaries of the church's traditional concern with "social justice." From the 1980s on, these issues have become more prominent in the church's advocacy, both nationally and at the state level. The touchstone for economic issues is the U.S. bishops' encyclical letter of 1986, *Economic Justice for All*, and the church's criminal justice advocacy has been bolstered by the increasingly negative view of the death penalty in the magisterial teaching of the church promoted during John Paul's papacy. Of the five top issues named by conference directors, health care is by far the least noticed by the general public. But as the ranking suggests, state Catholic conferences are dedicating an increasing amount of time and effort to the cause of health care, and especially the question of access to health care.

Critics may see this hierarchy as evidence of the bishops' obsession with the abortion issue (pro-life) and institutional self-defense (education) to the exclusion of other broader and equally valid concerns for social justice (economics, health care, criminal justice). Another way of understanding this hierarchy, however, is in terms of the extent to which "prudential judgment" is involved in translating the first-order moral principles of a religious tradition into second-, third-, and fourth-order political judgments on public policy options. This translation is not always straightforward. As the former editor of *First Things* James Nuechterlein has put it, "As a Christian, I believe that the most important thing I can say is that Christ is risen—when I am evangelizing. But there is very seldom an issue in the public square to which that is the appropriate answer."[11] Similarly, political philosopher Jeff Spinner-Halev has argued, "There are many issues that do not map onto religious beliefs. Should certain cities in New Jersey slow down their development? Should Congress pass campaign finance reform? Should health insurance pay for experimental bone-marrow transplants for cancer patients? Should interest rates be raised? One's belief that Christ died for our sins says little about these matters."[12] Getting from the death and resurrection of Jesus Christ to a position on sustainable growth, campaign finance reform, or interest rates requires prudential judgment.

According to the prominent Catholic legal scholar John T. Noonan, "No charism of infallibility protects the Church in judging contemporary men and issues. Infallibility is tied to the deposit of faith, not to the balancing of values almost always involved in specific policy judgements."[13] That balancing is the province of prudential judgment, in which honest disagreements can emerge. Not all public policy issues, however, require the same level of prudential judgment. Despite his cautionary note, Noonan also recognizes greater clarity on some specific policy positions: "That abortion itself is a grave sin is and has been the constant teaching of the Catholic church."[14] According to the *Catechism of the Catholic Church*, "Human life must be respected and protected absolutely from the moment of conception. . . . Since the first century, the Church has affirmed the moral evil of every procured abortion. This teaching has not changed and remains unchangeable."[15] Thus, for the bishops, and hence for the staff who advocate on their behalf in the state legislatures, little prudential judgment is required to derive a public policy position on abortion.[16] Similarly definitive is the church's teaching on education. The *Catechism* clearly outlines the church's view of the fundamental rights and responsibilities of parents with respect to their children, and particularly the education of their children: "The right and the duty of parents to educate their children are primordial and inalienable. . . . Parents have the first

responsibility for the education of their children. . . . As those first responsible for the education of their children, parents have the right to
choose a school for them which corresponds to their own convictions.
This right is fundamental. As far as possible parents have the duty of
choosing schools that will best help them in their task as Christian ed-
ucators. Public authorities have the duty of guaranteeing this parental
right and of ensuring the concrete conditions for its exercise."[17] Translating this teaching into an advocacy position is relatively straightforward for the conferences.[18]

The *Catechism* also speaks to the social doctrine of the church in
the area of economic activity, and particularly about what is called
"the preferential option for the poor."[19] According to the *Catechism*,
"those who are oppressed by poverty are the object of *a preferential
love* on the part of the Church which, since her origin and in spite of
the failings of many of her members, has not ceased to work for their
relief, defense, and liberation through numerous works of charity
which remain indispensable always and everywhere." The *Catechism*
points to various "juridical measures" that express this preference—
"the jubilee year of forgiveness of debts, prohibition of loans at interest and the keeping of collateral, the daily payment of the day-laborer,
the right to glean vines and fields"—but nowhere does it suggest the
best state policies to exercise the option for the poor.[20] Consequently,
although state Catholic conferences take social justice very seriously,
their advocacy positions on these types of issues—including economic justice, health care, and criminal justice—are less straightforward than on abortion and education. They require greater prudential judgment.

Sometimes, that judgment is left up to the professionals who staff
the conferences. Other times, the judgment is left up to the public officials who have been empowered to make political decisions for the
commonweal. As Christopher Dodson, executive director of the
North Dakota Catholic Conference, put it, "When addressing hunger,
is it better to have food stamps or something else? Those are really
matters of prudential judgment. One thing I know with my bishops is
that we will rarely step into matters of prudential judgment. Sometimes we will, but we make it clear that the bishops think it is so obvious that this is where we should go, based on our experience or
something like that. When we were working on health care reform in
North Dakota, we did not support any particular proposal here be-

cause, whether it's a single payer system or employee system or whatever, that's a matter of prudential judgment." John Huebscher, executive director of the Wisconsin Catholic Conference, took a similar approach to the health care issue: "When you get into the issue, for example, of access to health insurance, there are some people who don't want to talk about anything but a single payer system. Whereas I think that the church would say, there's a universal human right to health care, yet we respect the complexities of the issue enough *not* to prescribe a specific means of doing that. We know we don't have the expertise to do it, but we do know that we have a Gospel mandate to do it, and the resources exist for us to do it." In addressing a revenue shortfall in 2003, Nevada Catholic Conference executive director V. Robert Payant, also wanted to keep his advocacy at the level of principle: "I am preparing a statement by the bishops of Nevada, which I've already discussed with them, that will urge that sufficient revenues be raised to provide for the needs of education and welfare and corrections and so on. It is going to say that they have to rely on the wisdom of the legislature in deciding how to raise the revenues necessary, but the taxes should be fair and just. It isn't really weaseling because I have no idea what's the best tax bill, and I'm sure that the bishops don't either."

This is not to say that state Catholic conferences never advocate specific legislation on issues of economic justice, health care, or criminal justice. They do so all the time. But it is to recognize that there is less prudential judgment involved in responding to the Commandment "Thou shalt not kill" in the context of abortion legislation than there is in realizing the biblical mandate to "feed the hungry" in the context of a human services or state budget bill. This difference undergirds the hierarchy of issues pursued by state Catholic conferences.

The Importance of the Political Moment

As important as it is to understand the agenda and issue hierarchy of the Catholic bishops in America, it is equally important to understand how that agenda intersects with specific American political institutions at particular points in time. Although pro-life issues are clearly the top priority for most state Catholic conferences, that does not mean that in any given legislative session they will devote the most time to that issue. The example of the abortion issue in Utah is extreme but useful to illustrate the more general point. According to Dee Rowland, the legislative liaison for the statewide Diocese of Salt Lake City, "Because the LDS Church is very anti-abortion, I have the luxury of not having to spend time on abortion issues because the legislature is already pretty much there. I am not diminishing the importance of the abortion issue, but the fact that 98 percent of the legislators vote anti-abortion allows me to focus on other aspects of the seamless garment such as access to health care and adequate housing." Thus, when the church's comprehensive agenda is brought into the political arena by state Catholic conferences, it is transformed by the particular political situation in the state at the time.

A 28-year veteran of the Indiana state legislature as executive director of the Indiana Catholic Conference until he retired in 2004, M. Desmond Ryan knows this as well as anyone. Ryan emphasizes that "*the situation* will dictate what's a highlight at that moment." He continues,

> What's really important is *the moment*. So, if you are really for welfare reform and it is not an "*in*" issue, you talk, but you don't spend a lot of time on it. Same with abortion. And that is where it hurts, because for an anti-abortion person it's always the number one issue. But there are many times in the legislature—right before an election, for example— when those delicate issues are not going to be heard or not going to go anywhere. We just went through the budget cycle, so money is everything. You just do the best you can. Then you come into the next cycle, right before an election, and everything changes. On a pro-life bill, maybe they'll hear it and not take a vote, especially like right now when the House is divided 51 to 49. The Speaker of the House is with us as much as he can be. He's pro-life, pro–parochial schools. But when it's a short session, he doesn't want to put his 51 Democrats up on a bill that could affect the new elections. But you learn all those little nuances over time.

Ryan's sensitivity to "the moment" is driven in part by a political pragmatism born out of years of experience in the state legislative arena. It is also the product of the reality that the Indiana Catholic Conference has limited resources with which to do its work. As steward of those resources, Ryan must spend them carefully and wisely. Pursuing the abortion issue immediately prior to a major election in a closely divided legislature or pushing for public funding of private schools during a budget shortfall would not be a wise use of those resources.

Given resource limitations, state Catholic conferences need to pick and choose their battles carefully. Of all the legislation introduced in any given session, state Catholic conferences take an active interest in only a small percentage. Over 2,000 bills per session are introduced, on average, in legislatures where state Catholic conferences are active. Of those, state Catholic conferences on average *monitor* 127 bills. But of those bills being monitored, state Catholic conferences *give serious attention* to very few: just 31 bills, on average. And the average state Catholic conference *takes a public position* on only 22 bills per session. Experience working in the legislative system teaches the conferences that they must have some focus or risk being politically ineffective. The Florida Catholic Conference's associate for education, Larry Keough, stresses this in suggesting that "we have to make sure that there's a balance between monitoring all these bills and doing what we can to fulfill our legislative agenda. Since I've been here, there has usually been between a half-dozen and 10 goals that we're hoping to accomplish each year. That's our goal, but depending on the session and the dynamics of it, if we can get a couple of those, we feel fairly good." Keough continues,

> Say you're at an airport and you try to keep your eyes on eight people as you move around. Chances are you're going to lose them all. But if you spot one person and you keep your eyes fixed on that one person, chances are you're going to be able to follow that person around. Well, I think the same thing is true with the legislature. If you try to keep your eyes on 4,000 bills, you're not going to be able to do much of anything with any of them. So you need to prioritize and say, out of these 4,000 bills, realistically there are 20 that I'm going to devote 60 percent of my time to, and there are 10 that I'm going to devote 30 percent of my time to. The other 100 or 800 or 1,000 or 2,000? Well, I'll give them just a little bit of my time, maybe 10 percent, realizing that those are not priority issues. That's how I approach it. If I tried to be involved in-depth with all of the education bills that are filed, I don't think I'd be able to accomplish much of anything.

Of course, the Florida Catholic Conference is on the high end in terms of staff size, with 10 full-time equivalents. (The average conference has 4.5 FTEs.) Even these staff, however, are stretched thin by the extent and complexity of the public policy issues put before them by the Florida state legislature. As Keough concludes, with a rueful laugh, "Maybe there needs to be 7 people just for education, and 10 people for the life issues, and 8 people for social concerns. Obviously, you can make a bona fide case for having 40 people here, but that's just not going to happen. That's not the Catholic conference dynamic, so I won't even go there."

The political advocacy agenda of state Catholic conferences— grounded in the social teaching of the Catholic Church and representing a consistent ethic of life—is broad. As John Carr's grocery store encounter suggests, it may be absurdly broad. But the agendas actually pursued in the state legislative arena by Catholic conference staff are narrowed when the consistent life ethic is put into action. In the first place, there is a hierarchy of issues to which state Catholic conferences are committed. Overall, pro-life advocacy is a much higher priority than criminal justice. Furthermore, in many respects, state Catholic conferences are at the mercy of the political system. Because of their limited staffs, there is only so much they can hope to achieve in any given legislative session. Those aspirations are also limited by the realities of the political moment. These limitations notwithstanding, as we will see in the final section of this chapter, the consistent life ethic agenda can also be a political resource for state Catholic conferences.

NONPARTISANSHIP AS A POLITICAL RESOURCE

As the five top issues discussed above suggest, the advocacy of America's Roman Catholic bishops based on and encapsulated in the "consistent ethic of life" is orthogonal to the established liberal/conservative division that characterizes American political and cultural life today. The same cannot be said of Mainline and Evangelical Protestants, two theological traditions that map quite nicely onto the liberal/conservative political divide in the United States. As individuals, Mainline Protestants may be political centrists, as sociologists Robert Wuthnow and John Evans have suggested. But in their political advocacy, political scientist Laura Olson observes, Mainline organizations "have long advocated liberal political agendas."[21] Similarly, the orientation of individual Evangelicals to social change may stress the importance of personal influence over systematic engagement with the political system, as sociologist Christian Smith has argued. But in their political advocacy, Evangelical organizations do not shy away from seeking social reform geared at reasserting the conservative values of a "Christian America."[22] In stark partisan terms, the political agenda of Mainline Protestant organizations aligns with the Democratic Party agenda, and the political agenda of Evangelical Protestant organizations aligns with the Republican Party agenda.

The agendas of state Catholic conferences do not fit as easily into these dichotomies.[23] They alone crosscut the boundaries established by the partisan political system, taking conservative positions on issues of life and education, and liberal positions on issues of social and economic justice. This reality was key to Bernardin's conception of the "seamless garment." The fact is that the Catholic bishops of the United States are at times with the Democratic Party politically and at times with the Republican Party.[24] Given the increasing polarization of the American political system, not being aligned with one or the other major political party could be seen as a problem for the bishops. For example, political scientist Timothy Byrnes has observed, "The bishops are, at least in a collective sense, barred by the breadth and content of their agenda from the kind of close, organic relationships we have observed in recent years between other groups of clergy and one wing or another of the ideological spectrum."[25] But a nonpartisan agenda itself has political benefits, including being able to form relationships with politicians *across* the ideological spectrum.

Overwhelmingly, state Catholic conference staff see nonpartisanship not as a necessary evil, but as a political resource. Most importantly, it helps to bolster their moral legitimacy in the political arena. As North Dakota executive director Christopher Dodson suggests, "One of the best assets that we have is that we don't get involved in party politics, and therefore we have a respect and a certain amount of integrity that some organizations don't have." This is particularly important for state Catholic conferences because they see their moral legitimacy as their most important political resource. To wit, when surveyed about the most important resources they possess in their political advocacy work, 96 percent responded that their conference "possesses a reputation as a moral voice."[26] Having a political agenda closely aligned with one or the other political party is widely seen as compromising the moral high ground conferences seek to occupy.

Although they do not have as close relationships with legislators as some partisan political operatives, pursuing a nonpartisan political agenda requires state Catholic conferences to have and develop bi-partisan relationships with politicians. In the first place, the comprehensive agenda can open doors, and in the second place, it forces conference staff to reach out to a wide spectrum of politicians. According to Michael Sheedy, the Florida Catholic Conference's associate for health,

> When you look at the consistent ethic of life, we take positions that are both "conservative" and "liberal." There are some other religious groups that have enjoyed "up" times of late, but they rely very closely on the Republican majority and have very little to do with the minority Democrats. On the one hand, that is understandable and pragmatic, particularly in a state like ours, with a Republican legislature and governor. But on the other hand, they may not always have that Republican majority to work with. We can almost always find a place to begin a dialogue with legislators that is positive, which is a nice door opener, and I am glad we can do that before addressing issues in which we differ. For example, in our meeting last week with Representative Gibson, we were able to speak about our shared interest in expanding access to health care. This is an issue that has been a bigger priority for Democrats and is a huge issue for us. But when it comes to ensuring that we can provide health care in Catholic institutions that is within the boundaries of both our moral teachings and state law—a religious freedom issue with roots in our approach to moral issues—we get a lot more support from Republicans.

Sheedy concludes on a personal note, reflecting, "I hope that being consistent, fair-minded but firm, and relating across party lines earns us respect and advances the common good. On a personal level, I like having the sense I have that Gospel values provide some common ground with which to approach any legislator, and am very glad not to be completely identified with one party since someday the balance of power will change."

Other conference directors echoed Sheedy's sentiments and experiences when talking about putting a nonpartisan political agenda into action in a partisan political system. Desmond Ryan of the Indiana Catholic Conference maintains, "When we speak for the church, we're neither conservative nor liberal. We're issue oriented. And if you look at the consistent ethic theme of the Catholic Church, they're not Republican or Democratic issues, they're all over the place. The key is that we're welcome in any legislative office and any governor's office. I mean, one morning we're in a committee dealing with abortion with the conservative head of that committee, and in the after-noon, we're dealing with the welfare issue with a committee headed by a more liberal member. It just happens." Ryan concludes that "being a representative of the church is easy in the sense that they know our agenda is across the board. It's a plus. It really is a plus to me." A 30-year veteran of the Ohio Catholic Conference (including 16 years as executive director), Tim Luckhaupt sees the conference's relationships with legislators very positively. "I think we have good access to both parties here in the state—at the top levels with the speaker and the president of the Senate, who happen to be Republicans at this time. And then with the minority Democrats, I think we've got good lines of communication with them as well. On a lot of our issues, we garner fairly strong support across party lines. Obviously, it depends on what the issue is, but that's just a fact of the matter: you've got to work both sides of the aisle."

Reaching out to legislators from both political parties requires some flexibility in argumentation. What is convincing to a Democrat about an immigrant-rights bill, for example, will not necessarily be convincing to a Republican. But the comprehensiveness of the church's teachings and considerable practical experience working both sides of the aisle allows state Catholic conference staff to meet legislators where they are, to make arguments that will resonate with their particular background and beliefs. Ned Dolejsi, executive director of the California Catholic Conference, begins with the access he has to legislators of both parties. As he says, "From the Republican side, they know we are committed to life and family. From the Democratic side, they know we are committed to walking the journey with the poor, serving those in need, and helping immigrants." From there, he tailors his approach to the particular individual in question.

> You sit there, for example, and you know that this person is mostly concerned about the money or this person is mostly concerned about the impact on the future. If you start from where they're coming from, that certainly helps get their attention. So maybe I'm trying to talk with a legislator who traditionally votes against immigrant rights but is pro-life. I'm talking about why it's pro-life to vote for providing medical care to undocumented women with children—because the baby is still a baby. Whether it walked across [the border] by itself, or walked in the mother's womb, it's a baby, and you've got a responsibility here. So you can talk about that and get to that point. You know, there are times

when as Catholics we're asked by coalition members from the progressive end of things to talk to Republicans. The Republicans will see us
because of our commitment to life and family issues. And so we use
that as an entrée to get in and try to reframe the question that way.

And, of course, the opposite is true: using commitment to social justice as a point of entry into conversations with Democrats about life
and family issues. Sheila Hopkins, the associate for social concerns at
the Florida Catholic Conference, exemplifies this in her work.

When I visited Tallahassee in the spring of 2003, Hopkins was
working on number of pieces of legislation, including bills to increase
regulations on abortion clinics; abolish the death penalty for juve-
niles; facilitate adoption; and protect farm workers (by regulating pes-
ticides, mandating that contractors pay a minimum wage, and allowing undocumented aliens to receive in-state tuition at state
universities). These legislative priorities require her to lobby a wide
range of legislators from both parties. In seeing legislators, Hopkins
says, "I try to hit a note with each one, find something that they will
identify with." For example, when lobbying on a "Women's Health
and Safety Act," a pro-life bill that would increase regulations on abortion clinics, she visited a Democratic representative from West Palm
Beach. Hopkins argued to this legislator that the bill was not so much
about abortion as about women's health and the belief that "women
deserve better." Advocates of the bill maintain that regulations at
Florida's abortion clinics pale in comparison to other medical facilities. Regardless of the legislator's position on abortion or whether she
would want her daughter to have one, Hopkins maintained, she
would never want to get a call that her daughter died in the emergency room because of medical complications due to an abortion. Although the legislator ultimately voted against the bill in subcommit-
tee, Hopkins's desire to find a common cause with a legislator who
would not immediately be seen as a supporter is significant. California's Dolejsi concludes, and I'm sure Sheila Hopkins and other state
Catholic conference staff would agree, "I would talk to any legislator
over there. I wouldn't avoid any. Even with the ones who are antagonistic to us on other things, I try to find some common ground
around which we can talk. It's our job to open up those moments for
conversation." The consistent life ethic is seen as a valuable resource
in opening up those moments.

The inability to rely solely on one party also promotes badly needed civility in the political system. With very few exceptions, state Catholic conference staff do not "write off" any legislators as potential allies. As Dolejsi puts it, "You don't have any enemies. You can't afford to. You may need their help on another issue." Des Ryan of Indiana concurs: "I learned right from the beginning, you never have an enemy. You have a person who disagrees with you." R. Marie Hilliard of the Connecticut Catholic Conference expresses a similar view in slightly more dramatic terms: "Never demonize a person." Of course, this is true of all lobbyists, but it is particularly true of organizations that cannot align themselves with one party. Hilliard continues, "There are some legislators that I think highly of that are not with me on pro-life issues, but who went to the cross with me on protecting the seal of confession. I had one who spoke up for the death penalty at the same time that he was speaking against abortion. I know what I can ask of these legislators and what I can't ask of them. They say, Marie, you can always ask, even though I may tell you no."

That being professional religious advocates in a secular political system promotes civility was brought home for me when I was walking with D. Michael McCarron, executive director of the Florida Catholic Conference, from his office to the capitol building. On our way, we ran into another lobbyist with whom McCarron shared a friendly exchange, beginning with, "How you doin', Mike?" "Better than I deserve." "You got that right." After a moment, we walked away, and McCarron told me, "He's a lobbyist for the teacher's union." I expressed surprise at his cordial relationship with someone who has opposed the conference's goals on so many occasions. He replied, "Well, he doesn't have horns coming out of his head. Most lobbyists are good people. Even the ones from Planned Parenthood. You learn that from being here over time. We just have different philosophies." Of course, McCarron would not see all of these philosophies as equally valid, but the ability to recognize the humanity of one's foes seems to be a virtue in short supply in American politics. Upon further reflection, McCarron pointed to a passage in *Gaudium et Spes* as the guidance he tries to live by and convey to his colleagues at the Florida Catholic Conference: "Respect and love ought to be extended also to those who think or act differently than we do in social, political, or even religious matters. In fact, the more deeply we come to understand their ways of thinking through such courtesy and love, the more easily we will be able to enter into dialogue with them."[27]

CONCLUSION

The advocacy agenda of state Catholic conferences is best described as a nonpartisan, issue-based agenda centered on the dignity of the human person and the common good as the context within which that dignity can be realized. Although this "consistent ethic of life" treats issues from abortion and euthanasia to health care and poverty as part of a continuum, it does not equate them. State Catholic conference advocacy agendas reveal a clear hierarchy among these issues. Put metaphorically, not every thread in the "seamless garment" is of equal size or prominence. Furthermore, when the seamless garment is put into action, the political system conditions how conferences pursue their agendas and what they can hope to achieve. Under secular conditions, the Catholic Church cannot impose its agenda; it is more often reactive than proactive. State Catholic conferences must be sensitive to the political realities of the situation and take what the given institution will allow at that moment. Fortunately, the nonpartisan nature of the consistent life ethic provides ample opportunities for engagement across issues and party lines. But perhaps most importantly, it promotes state Catholic conferences' moral legitimacy and allows them to act as, in political scientist Clarke Cochran's words, "the pilgrim community's independent voice" in public life.[28]

NOTES

1. Jaroslav Pelikan, *The Melody of Theology: A Theological Dictionary* (Cambridge, MA: Harvard University Press, 1988), p. 252.

2. Biblical references for these teachings are as follows: the Beatitudes (Matthew 5:3–10), the Great Commandment (Luke 10:27); the rich man and Lazarus (Luke 16:19–31); and the rich young man (Mark 10:17–27).

3. Modern Catholic Social Teaching is roughly defined by a collection of key texts, including the following: the papal encyclicals *Rerum Novarum* (1891: "The Condition of Labor," Leo XIII), *Quadragesimo Anno* (1931: "After Forty Years," Pius XI), *Mater et Magistra* (1961: "Christianity and Social Progress," John XXIII), *Pacem in Terris* (1963: "Peace on Earth," John XXIII), *Popularum Progressio* (1967: "On the Development of Peoples," Paul VI), *Laborem Exercens* (1981: "On Human Work," John Paul II), *Sollicitudo Rei Socialis* (1987: "On Social Concern," John Paul II), and *Centes-*

imus Annus (1991: "On the Hundredth Anniversary of *Rerum Norvarum*," John Paul II); the papal letter *Octogesima Adveniens* (1965: "A Call to Action on the Eightieth Anniversary of Rerum Novarum," Paul VI); and the Second Vatican Council documents *Gaudium et Spes* (1965: "Pastoral Constitution on the Church in the Modern World") and *Dignitatis Humanane* (1965: "Declaration on Religious Freedom"). To these some would count as essential the 1971 Synod of Bishop's *Justice in the World*, Pope Paul VI's *Evangelii Nuntiandi* (1975: "Evangelization in the Modern World"), and two pastoral letters of the United States Catholic Bishops: *The Challenge of Peace: God's Promise and Our Response* (1983) and *Economic Justice for All* (1986). Excepting the Vatican II document on religious freedom, all of these documents are reprinted in David O'Brien and Thomas Shannon, eds., *Catholic Social Thought: The Documentary Heritage* (Maryknoll, NY: Orbis Books, 1992).

4. *The Social Encyclicals of John Paul II*, edited with introductions by J. Michael Miller, C.S.B. (Huntington, IN: Our Sunday Visitor, 1996).

5. Joseph Cardinal Bernardin, "A Consistent Ethic of Life: An American-Catholic Dialogue" (1983), pp. 7–16 in John Langan, S.J., ed., *A Moral Vision for America* (Washington, DC: Georgetown University Press, 1998), pp. 10, 12.

6. Joseph Cardinal Bernardin, "The Consistent Ethic of Life and Public Policy" (1988), pp. 51–58 in Langan, ed., *A Moral Vision for America*, p. 54.

7. Joseph Cardinal Bernardin, "Religion and Politics: Stating the Principles and Sharpening the Issues" (1984), pp. 37–50 in Langan, ed., *A Moral Vision for America*, pp. 44, 47.

8. Joseph Cardinal Bernardin, "The Consistent Ethic of Life: Its Theological Foundation, Its Ethical Logic, and Its Political Consequences," pp. 109–116 in Alphonse Spilly, ed., *Selected Works of Joseph Cardinal Bernardin: Church and Society*, vol. 2 (Collegeville, MN: Liturgical Press, 2000), p. 114; U.S. bishops' *Pastoral Plan for Pro-Life Activities: A Campaign in Support of Life* (United States Conference of Catholic Bishops, 2001), http://www.usccb.org/prolife/pastoralplan.htm (accessed 5 December 2004).

9. Weigel quoted in Joe Feuerherd, "Moral Values Largest Single Issue Cited by Electorate," *National Catholic Reporter*, 12 November 2004, p. 6. See an early critique by Michael Pakaluk, "A Cardinal Error: Does the Seamless Garment Make Sense?" pp. 196–204 in Charles Curran and Leslie Griffin, eds., *The Catholic Church, Morality, and Politics* (Mahwah, NJ: Paulist Press, 2001).

10. My survey was fielded in 2002, prior to the Massachusetts Supreme Judicial Court's November 2003 decision in *Goodridge v. Mass. Department of Public Health* (440 Mass. 309, 798 NE2d 941 [2003]), more commonly known

as Massachusetts' "gay marriage decision." According to the court, "Barred access to the protections, benefits, and obligations of civil marriage, a person who enters into an intimate, exclusive union with another of the same sex is arbitrarily deprived of membership in one of our community's most rewarding and cherished institutions. That exclusion is incompatible with the constitutional principles of respect for individual autonomy and equality under law." If I were to re-survey conference directors post-*Goodridge*, marriage and family issues could very well be among the top five issues listed.

11. George Weigel makes the distinction between orders of judgment in Michael Cromartie and Irving Kristol, eds., *Disciples and Democracy: Religious Conservatives and the Future of American Politics* (Washington, DC: Ethics and Public Policy Center, 1994), p. 35. Nuechterlein is quoted in *Disciples and Democracy*, p. 109.

12. Jeff Spinner-Halev, *Surviving Diversity: Religion and Democratic Citizenship* (Baltimore, MD: Johns Hopkins University Press, 2000), p. 149.

13. John T. Noonan Jr., "The Bishops and the Ruling Class: The Moral Formation of Public Policy," pp. 224–38 in Curran and Griffin, eds., *The Catholic Church, Morality, and Politics*, p. 226.

14. Noonan, "The Bishops and the Ruling Class," p. 235.

15. *Catechism of the Catholic Church*, rev. 2nd ed. (Washington, DC: United States Catholic Conference–Libreria Editrice Vaticana, 1997), nos. 2270, 2271.

16. Which is not to say that no choices need to be made in dealing with abortion as a public policy issue. As associate director of the Wisconsin Catholic Conference during the 1990s, Sharon Schmeling was primarily responsible for advocacy on pro-life issues. She characterizes her approach to abortion legislation as follows:

> It's a question of political realities. What are the political realities of the moment that are going to make what we want to happen possible? And so within that, there's deviation. But you're never deviating on your absolute principle. You're never saying, abortion is alright. You're saying, well, abortion is not alright, but on this day in this moment in history this is the best thing we can achieve for unborn children, so we're going to go after it. But we're going to do it in a way that legislators know that we think that it's not enough. Some people might view that as compromise, but the Holy Father's guidelines on imperfect legislation in *Evangelium Vitae* [The Gospel of Life] are helpful, to help people understand why that's not compromising—that sometimes in an imperfect world, on this side of the cross, given the fact that we're all tainted by original sin, getting a ban on partial birth abortion might be the best you can get. Would it be better to ban all abortion? You bet. But that's not politically feasible. So instead you go for what is politically feasible, and we work on that, and we take it one step at a time, all the while articulating our preferred position that all unborn life should be protected.

This prudential judgment about the best political *strategy* to take to advance the church's position, however, is not the same as a prudential judgment about the appropriate political *position* to take on an issue.

17. *Catechism of the Catholic Church*, nos. 2221, 2223, 2229, emphasis in original.

18. Even if the question of abortion and public policy is not straightforward in general. See R. Randall Rainey, S.J. and Gerard Magill, eds., *Abortion and Public Policy: An Interdisciplinary Investigation within the Catholic Tradition* (Omaha, NE: Creighton University Press, 1996).

19. For history and analysis of the concept, see Madeleine Adriance, *Opting for the Poor* (Kansas City, MO: Sheed & Ward, 1986) and Gustavo Gutiérrez, *A Theology of Liberation* (Maryknoll, NY: Orbis, 1973).

20. *Catechism of the Catholic Church*, nos. 2448, 2449.

21. Robert Wuthnow and John Evans, "Introduction," pp. 1–24 in Robert Wuthnow and John Evans, eds., *The Quiet Hand of God: Faith-Based Activism and the Public Role of Mainline Protestantism* (Berkeley: University of California Press, 2002), p. 21; Laura Olson, "Mainline Protestant Washington Offices and the Political Lives of Clergy," pp. 54–79 in Wuthnow and Evans, eds., *The Quiet Hand of God*, p. 55.

22. Christian Smith, *American Evangelicalism: Embattled and Thriving* (Chicago: University of Chicago Press, 1998), p. 187; see also Christian Smith, *Christian America? What Evangelicals Really Want* (Berkeley: University of California Press, 2000). But see Ralph Reed, "What Do Religious Conservatives Really Want?" pp. 1–15 in Michael Cromartie, ed., *Disciples and Democracy: Religious Conservatives and the Future of American Politics* (Washington, DC: Ethics and Public Policy Center, 1994).

23. Here I purposely limit my comments to episcopal conferences in recognition of the many Catholic groups whose political agendas are less comprehensive and hence more partisan. For example, NETWORK is a social justice lobby that takes exclusively those "liberal" positions that are the province of the Democratic Party (www.networklobby.org), and Priests for Life takes exclusively those "conservative" positions on pro-life issues that are the province of the Republican Party under the current political configuration in the United States (www.priestsforlife.org).

24. Whether the bishops are being pulled into a closer alignment with the Republican Party is a question I consider in the concluding chapter.

25. Timothy Byrnes, "American Church or Church in America? The Politics of Catholic Bishops in Comparative Perspective," pp. 120–38 in Sue Crawford and Laura Olson, eds., *Christian Clergy in American Politics* (Baltimore, MD: Johns Hopkins University Press, 2001), p. 134.

26. In the following chapter, I will argue that, in fact, state Catholic conferences have multiple bases of legitimacy, and in the short run, moral legitimacy may be their least important political resource. Following "reputation

as a moral voice," the following percentages of state Catholic conference directors reported possessing these different resources:

Expert knowledge	89%
Good connections to other organizations	82
Ability to mobilize members	79
Staff or facilities	71
Ability to mobilize public opinion	64
Reputation as an impartial mediator	36
Funds	25

27. Second Vatican Council, *Gaudium et Spes* ("Pastoral Constitution on the Church in the Modern World") (1965), no. 28.

28. Clarke Cochran, "The Pilgrim Community's Independent Voice," *America*, 3 December 2001, pp. 12–15.

4

Legitimacy

Political Influence and the Catholic Watergate

In November 2002, the Roman Catholic bishops of the United States gathered in Washington, as they do every fall, for the annual meeting of the United States Conference of Catholic Bishops (USCCB). These meetings are best known for the joint pastorals and statements the bishops vote on and issue to the Catholic faithful (and, occasionally, "to all people of goodwill"). It was at their fall meeting in 1983 that the bishops passed their landmark statement on nuclear war, *The Challenge of Peace*, and in 1986 their controversial and much-debated letter on the economy, *Economic Justice for All*. These statements, I have noted previously, solidified the position of the bishops as a leading moral voice on sociopolitical issues in the United States.

In the ballroom of the Hyatt Regency on Capitol Hill, the 200-plus bishops present in 2002 continued their tradition of considering pressing issues inside and outside the church and lending their voice to public debate by issuing statements. On November 13, the USCCB issued four major documents: *When I Call for Help: A Pastoral Response to Domestic Violence against Women*; *Encuentro and Mission: A Renewed Pastoral Framework for Hispanic Ministry*; *A Place at the Table: A Catholic Recommitment to Overcome Poverty and to Respect the Dignity of All God's Children*; and, most notably, a *Statement on Iraq*. This last statement reiterated concerns about a possible U.S.-led invasion of Iraq expressed by USCCB president Bishop Wilton Gregory in a letter of September 13, 2002, to President George W. Bush. It expressed "fear that resort to war, under present circumstances and

101

in light of current public information, would not meet the strict conditions in Catholic teaching for overriding the strong presumption against the use of military force." As before, the public reception of these statements would be taken as a measure of the bishops' status in the American public square.

Of these statements, only the *Statement on Iraq* received immediate press coverage. Even that was not, as journalists say, "above the fold." It was not given major coverage. To wit, the *New York Times* buried its story on the statement on page 31 ("War on Iraq Not Yet Justified, Bishops Say"), and the *Washington Post*'s story ran on page 29 ("Catholic Bishops: War with Iraq Hard to Justify"). The demotion of this statement might be taken as evidence of a lack of interest in Catholic affairs among members of the Fourth Estate. But in fact, the *Times* ran lead stories—page 1, column 1, above the fold—on the Catholic Church three times during the week of the bishops' meeting:

- "Scandal is Stirring Lay Catholics to Push Church for More Power" (Sunday, November 10)
- "Cardinal Law's New Approach to Abuse Cases" (Wednesday, November 13)
- "Bishops Pass Plan to Form Tribunals in Sex Abuse Cases" (Thursday, November 14)

One did not need to travel long down the road of Catholicism in the United States in 2002 before crossing paths with the clergy sexual abuse scandal.

In January 2002, the *Boston Globe* began running a series of investigative articles on the sexual abuse of children by priests and the mishandling of those priests by bishops in the Archdiocese of Boston. From that point on, one could not mention the Catholic Church in public without in the same breath lamenting "*the scandal.*" The year 2002 would come to be thought of by some as the "*annus horribilis*"; it would be "etched in the collective memory of Catholics as the year of hideous truth."[1] Most commentators saw the situation as being historic in proportion. According to George Weigel, a Catholic theologian and fellow of the Ethics and Public Policy Center, "In the first months of 2002, the Catholic Church in the United States entered the greatest crisis in its history." Historian Jay Dolan concurred: "There has been nothing like this in the history of American Catholicism."[2]

Among the saddest aspects of the case of John Geoghan in Boston—whose trial started the wave of attention that subsequently washed over the entire United States—is that his was not the first case of sexual abuse of children by a priest to garner national attention. In the 1980s, there was Fr. Gilbert Gauthe of Lafayette, Louisiana, famously profiled by Jason Berry in his 1992 book *Lead Us Not into Temptation: Catholic Priests and the Sexual Abuse of Children.* In the 1990s, there was Archbishop Robert Sanchez of Santa Fe, New Mexico; Fr. James Porter of Fall River, Massachusetts; and Fr. Rudy Kos of Dallas, Texas. In 2000, Fr. Andrew Greeley wrote that the story Berry uncovered "may be the greatest scandal in the history of religion in America and perhaps the most serious crisis Catholicism has faced since the Reformation." This same sentiment would be repeatedly expressed two years later concerning the scandal emanating from Boston. And Berry's diagnosis of the problem in 1992 could be reprinted verbatim a decade later without seeming dated at all: "The crisis in the Catholic Church lies not with the fraction of priests who molest youngsters but in an ecclesiastical power structure that harbors pedophiles, conceals other sexual behavior patterns among its clerics, and uses strategies of duplicity and counterattack against its victims."[3] In this sense, the 12,000 sex-abuse-by-priests stories that had been carried by major print and broadcast news sources by the time of the bishops' June 2002 meeting in Dallas were not really covering "news." As Peter Steinfels, who was senior religion correspondent for the *New York Times* from 1988 to 1997, describes his reaction to the revelations of 2002, "I was not seeing a new wave of post-1993 sexual abusers. I was seeing the same wave—risen, as it were, from the grave."[4]

This historical amnesia notwithstanding, Catholics from the theological left to the theological right stressed the historical significance of the sexual abuse crisis of 2002, comparing it to the Watergate scandal that brought down the Nixon administration. "This is our Catholic Watergate," declared Tom Beaudoin, author of *Virtual Faith: The Irreverent Spiritual Quest of Generation X*, "an unholy brew of duplicity and desecration, sealed sickeningly by desperate clergy with threats of hell—from Cardinal Bernard F. Law calling down God's wrath on the media to priests who scared boys with threats of eternal damnation for breaking silence." Similarly, William Donohue, president of the church-defending Catholic League for Religious and Civil Rights, said, "This is the Catholic Church's Watergate, and these wounds are entirely self-inflicted. This has nothing to do with anti-Catholicism in the media or anyplace else. The Catholic Church is wholly to blame for this dereliction of duty, the collapse of standards. And I don't think it's any mistake as a believing, practicing Catholic that this series of events unfolded during Lent."[5] Without getting too carried away with the comparison—after all, unlike Watergate, the immediate victims of the Catholic scandal were children[6]—the similarities between the two cases are striking. Both involved illegal, conspiratorial behavior, behavior that was surely immoral where it was not technically illegal, behavior that was subsequently covered up by superiors and that led to the resignation of the chief officer responsible (after some delay, Cardinal Law ultimately resigned on December 13, 2002).

As the Watergate scandal 30 years earlier negatively affected respect for governmental institutions,[7] the sexual abuse scandal in the Catholic Church precipitated a decline in respect for the authority of religious institutions. In a poll released in June 2002, George Gallup Jr. found confidence in organized religion in the United States at its lowest level in six decades, a decline Gallup attributed directly to the scandal in the Catholic Church. In 2001, prior to the scandal becoming public, 60 percent of Americans had "a great deal" or "quite a lot" of confidence in organized religion. The following year, that proportion had dropped to 45 percent. The level of confidence was far lower among Catholics (42 percent) than Protestants (59 percent). These data led Gallup to conclude, "This is strictly a Catholic phenomenon. There's very little rub-off or collateral damage done to Protestants."[8]

The full implications of this crisis will take some time to play and sort themselves out, but the Gallup Poll data suggest some effects were more immediately evident. Of particular interest here are the political implications of the scandal. Indeed, there was considerable hand-wringing among Catholics about the negative effects of the "Great Lenten Humiliation" (Richard John Neuhaus's phrase) on the political influence of the church. As historian Dolan wrote in a postscript to his 2002 book *In Search of an American Catholicism*,

> As Catholicism has become a more public, less insular religion, church leaders have addressed such topics as war and peace, the economy, abortion, and the death penalty. By speaking out, they assumed an important moral authority in the public discussion of these critical social issues. The duplicity and cover-up on the part of many bishops has severely damaged, if not destroyed, that authority, and it will take more

than just apologies to restore the credibility lost in the revelations of the winter and spring of 2002.[9]

Dolan's concerns were echoed by many in the church. In his annual address at the Catholic Charities USA membership meeting in August 2002, CCUSA president Fr. Bryan Hehir asked, "How will we sustain our public voice—an essential part of the Church's ministry?" That same month, Bishop William Skylstad of Spokane declared, "Our moral credibility, effectiveness and leadership will likely be diminished as long as this shadow hangs over us."[10]

For some, the low ebb politically was when the bishops' *Statement on Iraq* was totally eclipsed in the media by their revised *Charter for the Protection of Children and Young People*. At the end of the bishops' fall meeting, Rev. Canice Connors, president of the Conference of Major Superiors of Men, told the *Washington Post*, "Of course the bishops feel the loss of their status to speak on these [public] issues. We all feel it. That's the big loss from this scandal." Early in 2003, the *New York Times* summarized the sentiments of many inside and outside the church in an article entitled "Testing the Church's Influence in Politics." "The influence of American bishops in the broader political debate stems largely from their moral authority," the article observes. It then asserts, "This moral authority has almost certainly been diminished by the church's handling of the sex abuse scandals."[11]

These concerns and assertions about the implications of the Catholic Watergate for the public role of the bishops raises an important question: What *are* the bases of the bishops' political legitimacy and influence? I suggest two answers. First, working through the agency structure of state Catholic conferences, the bishops have multiple bases of legitimacy. Second, moral authority is one of these bases, but the way it works is not how people commonly assume. By elaborating these answers, this chapter helps explain why the bishops' political influence in the "Long Lent of 2002" (Neuhaus, again) did not suffer nearly as much as many observers had feared or hoped.

THE VARIABLE EFFECTS OF THE SCANDAL

Before assuming the bird's-eye view of the analyst, we do well to spend some time on the front lines, in the trenches with state Catholic conferences in the 2002 and 2003 legislative sessions. Doing so, we find that the scandal did have specific, identifiable political effects. This was especially true in two areas of public policy: extending the statute of limitations for civil child sexual abuse actions and including clergy as mandatory reporters of child abuse. We saw this in the case of the Maryland General Assembly in chapter 1. While the Maryland Catholic Conference was successful in promoting legislation on these issues that was acceptable to the church and in opposing legislation that was not, not all state Catholic conferences were as fortunate.

In the most extreme case, the president of the California State Senate sponsored legislation during the 2002 legislative session to *suspend entirely* for one year (January 1–December 31, 2003) the statute of limitations on civil actions to recover damages for childhood sexual abuse. Although it was clearly targeted at the Catholic Church, the bishops of the state could not publicly oppose the bill given the hostile climate that prevailed in the legislature at the time. In two committee and three floor votes, the legislation passed by a cumulative margin of 160 to 0. As a consequence, the church in California faces several hundred civil suits, some dating as far back as the 1930s.[12] A close second behind California is Connecticut, which enacted legislation in 2002 to extend the statute of limitations in cases of child sexual abuse from 2 to 30 years from the date the victim attains the age of majority (i.e., from 20 years old to 48 years old) for criminal cases, and from 17 to 30 years from the age of majority in civil cases, and it made these new limits *retroactive*. As in California, the bishops in Connecticut did not publicly oppose these measures.[13]

A second area of legislation that was animated by the scandal was adding clergy to the list of mandatory reporters of child maltreatment (including sexual abuse). It should be noted that the construction of child maltreatment as a social problem to be addressed in criminal and civil law is a relatively recent phenomenon. In America, Henry Bergh founded the Society for the Prevention of Cruelty to Animals in 1866, almost a decade before he helped found the Society for the Prevention of Cruelty to Children in 1875. As law professor Karen Ross succinctly puts it, "child abuse is not a new phenomenon, though its recognition and punishment is." Consequently, laws regarding child abuse have only been developed over the past four decades. The key moment in this development was the publication in 1962 of a paper by Dr. C. Henry Kempe that elaborated the idea of "battered child syndrome" and recommended that physicians be required to report child abuse. In 1963, the Children's Bureau of the Department of Health, Education and Welfare created a model child-abuse reporting statute, and by 1967 every state had enacted statutes that included physicians as mandatory reporters of physical abuse.[14]

Since then, every state has amended its reporting statute at least once to expand the list of mandatory reporters and the types of reportable abuse (from physical abuse to physical, mental, emotional, and sexual abuse and neglect variously defined). The professionals most commonly named in state statutes as mandatory reporters are medical personnel, mental health professionals, social workers, school personnel, law enforcement officers, and child care providers. By the mid-1980s, clergy in four states were named as mandatory reporters. In 1971, Connecticut added "clergyman" to its list. Nevada also named "clergyman" as a mandatory reporter, while Mississippi included "minister," and New Hampshire listed "priest, minister, or rabbi." This inclusion of clergy (broadly understood) raised the issue of the professional privilege sometimes granted to clergy and those who come to them for spiritual counseling. So, for example, the Nevada statute included the following exemption from clergy reporting: "unless he has acquired the knowledge of the abuse or neglect from the offender during a confession."[15]

The National Clearinghouse on Child Abuse and Neglect Information notes, "As a doctrine of some faiths, clergy have an obligation to maintain the confidentiality of pastoral communications. . . . The privilege of maintaining this confidentiality under State law must be provided by statute, and most States do provide the privilege in statute, typically in rules of evidence of civil procedure," when not in the reporting law itself.[16] When state legislators began looking at the issue of clergy as mandatory reporters of child abuse and neglect in response to the church scandal in 2002, the most pressing concern for state Catholic conferences was protecting clergy-penitent privilege, a centuries-old tradition in the church. According to Mary Harter Mitchell, the privilege claimed by all clergy

> originated in the seal of confession of the Roman Catholic church. For centuries, the Catholic seal of confession has protected as inviolably secret the contents of a penitent's auricular confession to a priest. Although historians have not located a precise origin for the seal, they have found references to the practice of secrecy from early records of the Christian

church. In the fifth century, Pope Leo I acknowledged an already long-standing practice of secret confession, and in the ninth century, church law imposed punishment on any priest who violated the seal.[17]

The 1983 Code of Canon Law includes excommunication as a punishment for a priest violating the seal of confession (canons 983, no. 1, and 1388, no. 1).

Table A.4 in appendix A offers an overview of the status of clergy as mandatory reporters before and after the scandal broke in January 2002. Table A.4 shows that, prior to the scandal, 12 states specifically included clergy as mandatory reporters of child abuse, and 17 more included clergy in other categories (e.g., "any person"). These 29 states maintained an exemption for clergy privileged communications. Sometimes this exemption is given in the reporting statute itself, as we have already seen in the case of Nevada. In other cases, the exemption is given in the state's rules of evidence or civil procedure (typically not requiring clergy to testify regarding privileged information). For example, Rule 505 of the Texas Rules of Evidence reads,

(a) Definitions. As used in this rule: (1) A "member of the clergy" is a minister, priest, rabbi, accredited Christian Science Practitioner, or other similar functionary of a religious organization or an individual reasonably believed so to be by the person consulting with such individual; (2) A communication is "confidential" if made privately and not intended for further disclosure except to other persons present in furtherance of the purpose of the communication; (b) General Rule of Privilege. A person has a privilege to refuse to disclose and to prevent another from disclosing a confidential communication by the person to a member of the clergy in the member's professional character as spiritual adviser; (c) Who May Claim the Privilege. The privilege may be claimed by the person, by the person's guardian or conservator, or by the personal representative of the person if the person is deceased. The member of the clergy to whom the communication was made is presumed to have authority to claim the privilege but only on behalf of the communicant.

In contrast, Mississippi requires clergy to report without exemption for privileged communications, and North Carolina, Oklahoma, and Tennessee require any person to report with no clergy-penitent privilege. (Note that these are four of the states in which there is no state Catholic conference established.)

At the start of 2002, 18 states did not address clergy reporting specifically, and it was in these states that the legislatures acted most quickly to redress the situation. For example, the scandal came to Missouri most prominently in the form of Bishop Anthony O'Connell, then of Palm Beach, Florida. O'Connell was accused in March 2002 of sexually assaulting underage students in the 1970s while he was rector of St. Thomas Aquinas Seminary in Hannibal, Missouri. This story brought calls to include clergy as mandatory reporters of suspected child abuse or neglect. In the end, such legislation was enacted, but not until an exemption was secured by Rev. Mr. Lawrence Weber, executive director of the Missouri Catholic Conference, for "privileged communication made to [a minister] in his or her professional capacity." The outcome in Missouri is typical of state Catholic conferences' handling of the issue. There was no objection to including clergy as mandatory reporters as long as the clergy-penitent privilege was not abrogated. In one case, Michigan, the Catholic Conference actually took the lead in getting legislation on the books that would include clergy as mandatory reporters with privilege. Michigan's vice president for public policy, Paul Long, describes the process:

> Given the controversy and the scandal which raged last year with regard to child sexual abuse, there were rumblings in the state capital that clergy had never been a part of the list to report suspected abuse and that they ought to be a part of that list of professions. Traditionally, the Michigan Catholic Conference has opposed adding clergy to the list from the standpoint of First Amendment concerns with regard to the rites of the confessional. So, when we began to hear rumblings early last spring that there was going to be something introduced when the legislature returned from their Easter recess, we decided that if we were going to be in the face of an oncoming freight train we should get our own train. So we went to a couple of folks in the legislature who we have great respect for. We asked them if they would be willing to sponsor legislation along these lines and provided them with the language that we felt would be helpful to them in drafting such a bill.

The resulting bill passed the Michigan House without a dissenting vote in June 2002, and was passed unanimously in December 2002 by the Michigan Senate. Though the bill went through several rewrites, according to Long,

> It was our belief all along that the bill did three things. It helped to protect children in a greater way, because another profession was going to be required to report suspected abuse. It also provided that those who

abuse children would be reported on. There was a section that provides that, while anyone can be reported on, there are a couple of specific professions which can be reported on, and we've added clergy to that. But the legislation also protected the rite of confession. It protected the right of confidential conversation between members of the clergy and the people that come to them for such conversation.

As table A.4 shows, every statutory change in 2002 and 2003 to include clergy as mandatory reporters granted an exemption for privileged clergy communications.

In contrast, in every state in which legislation was proposed that would require clergy to violate the seal of confession (as in Connecticut, Kansas, Kentucky, and Maryland), the proposals were defeated (see table A.4), in large part because of the work of state Catholic conferences.[18] As with the Maryland Catholic Conference, I observed the Florida Catholic Conference successfully addressing this issue as well. During my spring 2003 visit to Tallahassee, Executive Director D. Michael McCarron and Associate Director for Health Michael Sheedy had a "meet and greet" appointment with a freshman legislator from the Jacksonville area. Sheedy made the appointment to introduce himself and the Florida Catholic Conference to her. The meeting was particularly important for Sheedy because the legislator is from a Catholic family and has strong ties to a Catholic hospital in Jacksonville. McCarron came along because this legislator was the sponsor of a bill to add clergy to the list of mandatory reporters of child sexual abuse without privilege for priest-penitent communications. During the meeting, McCarron gave her a copy of the diocesan guidelines for handling child sexual abuse that were passed by the Florida bishops in December 2002. He wanted to impress upon her that the church in Florida was taking steps to address the problem. He also raised the issue of the seal of confession in the sacrament of reconciliation and commended to her another bill before the legislature that would make clergy mandatory reporters and protect the seal of confession at the same time. She seemed to be unaware of the problem in the bill she was sponsoring and was receptive to McCarron's concern. McCarron's quiet lobbying and behind-the-scenes organizing, aided to be sure by Florida's severe budget shortfall and other pressing legislative initiatives, was enough to ensure that none of these bills were enacted by the legislature in 2003.

Even when the legislative outcome was desirable, however, the opportunity costs of addressing legislation on the statute of limitations and clergy reporting—in terms of time, energy, and political capital—were considerable. The privileged communication exemption to the mandatory reporting law in Missouri, which clearly protects the seal of confession, was the major accomplishment of the 2002 legislative session for the Missouri Catholic Conference, a fact Executive Director Weber was not particularly proud of. In his words, "I had to turn my back on a positive legislative package and turn my attention to this thing that had fallen into my lap." The staff of the Wisconsin Catholic Conference expressed similar sentiments. People in the Wisconsin state legislative arena "understand we have this problem. They understand that we've taken some hits," says Executive Director John Huebscher. At the same time, "People were not reluctant to ask us to be at press conferences last spring around stem cell research and cloning. People were not reluctant to enlist us in support of efforts to keep the death penalty illegal or to advocate for programs for needy people. So in terms of our legislative advocacy, I don't sense that it's been a big problem." What, then, was the primary effect of the scandal? According to Huebscher, "I think the primary effect it has had on the work we do is the time it has taken us to deal with the anticipated legislative response to it. I've spent time that I would not have spent in other years understanding liability law and discerning how we're going to engage the legislature in terms of responding to some of the changes that victims and survivors and others want the legislature to make." This is born out in the Wisconsin Catholic Conference's lobbying report for the first quarter of 2003. The conference reports spending 25 percent of its lobbying efforts between January and June 2003 on a single issue: sexual misconduct by clergy.[19]

The opportunity costs of engaging legislation on scandal-related issues notwithstanding, many state Catholic conferences had some public policy successes to report in 2002. Iowa, for example, became just the second state in the country to ban human cloning in April 2002 when Governor Tom Vilsack signed the Human Cloning Prohibition Act. The cloning ban bill was introduced and advocated in the legislature by the staff of the Iowa Catholic Conference, with considerable assistance from Richard Doerflinger of the USCCB's Secretariat for Pro-Life Activities. "We had never worked so hard on an issue before," Executive Director Sara Eide recalls. "Cloning is a very

complicated moral and legal issue, and although the bill passed easily in the Senate, we still had to talk to every senator about it. Of
course, before I was in a position to educate the legislators on a
cloning ban, I needed to get up to speed on the issue myself. In the
end, there were some legislators who I spent hours talking to because they were really struggling with it. As the bill worked its way
through the legislature, we were working 15 or 16 hours every day
trying to get it passed." These long hours paid off in the end. Clearly,
from its introduction to the final passage of the bill, the Iowa
Catholic Conference was the prime mover of the legislation.

Also in 2002, health care payers in Oregon received a broad conscience exemption in the state's Medicaid waiver from the federal
government's Center for Medicare and Medicaid Services. Under the
waiver, a health care payer providing services "is not required to provide, pay for, make available or make a referral for a service to an individual receiving health care . . . if the health care payer objects to
the provision of that service on the basis of religious beliefs, moral
convictions or conscience." After an unsuccessful attempt to include
this conscience clause in Oregon's Family Health Insurance Assistance Program in 2001, the Oregon Catholic Conference turned to the
federal government. The exemption was worked into Oregon's Medicaid contract by Executive Director Robert Castagna, who worked
closely with the staff of the USCCB's offices of government liaison,
pro-life activities, and general counsel. Castagna characterized the effort as "a prized moment . . . in terms of USCCB and state Catholic
conference collaboration."

In Pennsylvania, the Catholic conference led the effort to pass the
Religious Freedom Protection Act, designed to restore the "compelling state interest" standard removed by the U.S. Supreme Court
in their 1990 decision in *Employment Division v. Smith* and their
1997 decision in *Boerne v. Flores* (which struck down the federal
Religious Freedom Restoration Act). The legislation passed by wide
margins in both houses of the legislature—this despite the fact that
the ACLU of Pennsylvania tried to play "the scandal card" during the
debate by accusing the Pennsylvania Catholic Conference of advo-
cating the legislation in order to shield pedophile priests from legal
accountability. This legislation had been a priority of the Pennsylvania Conference for some time and ironically only "got legs" in the
year of the Catholic Watergate.

All of these reports from the political front point to what social scientists might (accurately but inelegantly) call "the variable effects of the scandal." Despite the dire predictions of some observers, Catholic bishops did not lose all of their political legitimacy and influence during the Long Lent of 2002. My primary purpose in the balance of this chapter, then, is to suggest why the bishops were not as politically compromised as many commentators asserted or assumed. As the examples given above suggest, it has to do with the structure and operation of state Catholic conferences.

DUAL STRUCTURES AND MULTIPLE BASES OF LEGITIMACY

As interest groups, state Catholic conferences are part of the same organizational environment as teachers unions, chambers of commerce, bankers associations, manufacturers associations, organized labor, utility companies and associations, state bar and trial lawyers associations, municipal leagues and counties associations, and state farm bureaus. Studies of interest groups consistently rank these organized interests as the most effective in lobbying state government.[20] Examining the most "effective" advocacy organizations reveals certain characteristics they possess that are beyond the reach of state Catholic conferences.

First of all, the most effective lobbying organizations spend far more time and money lobbying than other interest groups. Consider the data from the Wisconsin state legislature given in table 4.1. In the 2001–2002 biennium, 678 organizations registered to lobby with the Wisconsin State Ethics Board. But the top 11 organized interests, from the Forest County Potawatomi Community to Philip Morris, accounted for 20 percent of all lobbying expenditures. Although the Wisconsin Catholic Conference spends more time and money lobbying than the average organization in Wisconsin, it spends far less than the biggest-spending and most influential groups.

Moreover, the most effective lobbies typically establish political action committees (PACs) to make campaign donations to candidates, parties, or other PACs. They often endorse candidates for public office, as well (see table 4.2 for the extent of this interest group activity at the state and federal levels). In his survey of interest group politics in Wisconsin, Ronald Hedlund writes, "the Wisconsin Education

Table 4.1.   Top Lobbying Organizations in Wisconsin and Wisconsin Catholic Conference Compared

Organization	# Registered Lobbyists	# Hours Lobbying	Total Lobbying Expenditures
Forest Co. Potawatomi Community	5	2,794	$1,371,509
WI Education Association Council	22	9,411	1,117,838
WI Manufacturers & Commerce	12	10,296	1,103,216
WI Independent Businesses	2	13,643	967,503
WI Merchants Federation	2	7,111	914,489
WI Counties Association	12	11,478	689,894
WI Energy Corporation	18	2,922	667,914
WI Farm Bureau Federation	3	7,427	602,108
WI Health and Hospital Assn.	14	5,063	598,469
Ameritech (WI Bell, Inc.)	8	4,464	592,429
Philip Morris	6	1,632	562,934
Wisconsin Catholic Conference	3	1,886	94,206
State Average	—	656	68,731

Source: State of Wisconsin Ethics Board, "Lobbying Effort in 2001–2002," http://ethics.state.wi.us/ LobbyingRegistrationReports/LobbyingOverview.htm (accessed 21 July 2003). Registered lobbyists include in-house and contract lobbyists.

Association Council (WEAC) is generally reputed to be one of the most effective special interest groups, if not the most effective, in the state." Not surprisingly, in addition to the million-plus dollars they spent on lobbying in 2001–2002, the WEAC PAC also spent $156,000 on state elections in the 2002 election cycle, making it one of the top campaign contributors in the state.[21] As an organization exempt from federal income tax under section 501(c)(3) of the Internal Revenue Code, the Catholic Church is prohibited from engaging in this sort of political campaign activity.[22] State Catholic conferences are covered by the blanket IRS tax exemption for Catholic organizations listed in the *Official Catholic Directory* and are therefore subject to these limitations on their political activity.

Legitimacy and Legislative Sausage-Making

State Catholic conferences, however, are not entirely without bases of legitimacy and influence in the public policy arena. In chapter 2, I introduced the idea that from a sociological perspective state Catholic conferences are best understood as *dual structures*. As such, much of the political legitimacy and influence of the bishops comes not from the authority structure's prophetic voice calling out in the wilderness, but through the agency structure's intimate involvement in the messy world of legislative politics. Although they cannot engage in electoral politics directly, state Catholic conferences make use of a wide range of other interest group lobbying techniques. In fact, state Catholic conferences are *more* likely than interest groups as a whole, both at the state and federal levels, to utilize 10 of the 18 lobbying techniques enumerated in Kay Schlozman and John Tierney's landmark research on organized interests in Washington, D.C. (see table 4.2). Ninety

Table 4.2. Percentage of Organizations Using Various Lobbying Techniques (Rank in Parentheses)

Technique	State Catholic Conferences	State Data	Federal Data
Testifying at legislative hearings	100 (1)	99 (1)	99 (1)
Helping to draft legislation	97 (T2)	88 (4)	85 (T5)
Attempting to shape implementation of policies	97 (T2)	85 (6)	89 (3)
Inspiring letter-writing or telegram campaigns	97 (T2)	83 (T8)	84 (T7)
Consulting with government officials to plan legislative strategy	90 (T5)	84 (7)	85 (T5)
Talking with people from the media	90 (T5)	74 (13)	86 (4)
Having influential constituents contact their legislators	87 (T7)	92 (3)	80 (T9)
Mounting grass-roots lobbying efforts	87 (T7)	86 (5)	80 (T9)
Shaping the government's agenda by raising new issues and calling attention to previously ignored problems	87 (T7)	83 (T8)	84 (T7)
Alerting state legislators to the effects of a bill on their districts	84 (T10)	94 (2)	75 (13)
Helping to draft regulations, rules, or guidelines	84 (T10)	81 (T10)	78 (11)
Engaging in informal contacts with officials	84 (T10)	81 (T10)	95 (2)
Serving on advisory committees and boards	74 (13)	76 (12)	76 (12)
Doing favors for officials who need assistance	58 (14)	36 (17)	56 (16)
Filing suit or otherwise engaging in litigation	45 (15)	40 (16)	72 (14)
Engaging in protests and demonstrations	36 (16)	21 (T20)	20 (21)
Attempting to influence appointment to public office	26 (17)	42 (15)	53 (17)
Running advertisements in the media	20 (18)	21 (T20)	31 (18)
Making monetary contributions to candidates	—	45 (14)	58 (15)
Working on election campaigns	—	29 (18)	24 (19)
Endorsing candidates	—	24 (19)	22 (20)

Sources: 2002 State Catholic Conference Survey. State data from Anthony Nownes and Patricia Freeman, "Interest Group Activity in the States," *Journal of Politics* 60 (February 1998):86-112, Table 2. Federal data from Kay Lehman Schlozman and John Tierney, "More of the Same: Washington Pressure Group Activity in a Decade of Change," *Journal of Politics* 45 (1983):351-77, Table 1.

percent or more of state Catholic conferences testify at legislative hearings, help to draft legislation, attempt to shape implementation of policies, inspire letter-writing or telegram campaigns, consult with government officials to plan legislative strategy, and talk with people from the media.

This level of involvement in the public policy process by state Catholic conferences departs considerably from the view of religious lobbying offered by political scientist Allen Hertzke in his landmark study *Representing God in Washington.* Hertzke observes that religious advocacy groups in general are often reluctant or ill equipped to engage in the "detail work," the "micro-process," the "sausage-making," which is central to the legislative process.[23] Not so the state Catholic conferences. Conference directors realize involvement in legislative sausage-making presumes and reinforces a group's political legitimacy. Political legitimacy can be defined roughly as the right to speak, be heard, and be taken seriously in the political process. Political advocates themselves prefer the term *credibility.* Credibility in the legislative process is built up slowly over time and, in the case of state Catholic conferences, adheres more to the agency than to the authority structure. A key source of state Catholic conferences' influence is the political credibility that comes from the staff, particularly the executive director, having relationships with policy makers, providing them useful information, and telling the truth.

As we saw in chapter 2, a background in state government is increasingly important for state Catholic conference directors. When Sara Eide moves from the Senate majority leader's office to the Iowa Catholic Conference, or Michael Farmer gives up his seat in the Kansas House of Representatives to lead the Kansas Catholic Conference, or Ronald Johnson begins representing the Arizona Catholic Conference instead of the State Bar of Arizona, the relationships they have developed in their previous work carry over to their new positions. As Eide puts it, "What I need to do my job effectively is to have relationships with legislators. I need them to know who I am, to get along with me, and to trust me." Among Eide's advantages from having worked in the legislature previously is "being friends with staff members on both sides [Republicans and Democrats] and with the nonpartisan staff. It is especially helpful to know who to go to for help on different issues. These staff have been a great help to me." Robert O'Hara brought 19 years of experience lobbying for a local utility in Pennsylvania to his work at the Catholic conference there. As he explains his situation, "The guy who I followed was a bit of a legend. People knew him. He had a good reputation. And I was pretty well-known, too. After 19 years, people know you."

This comment points to the fact that relationships, and the credibility associated with them, are frequently built up over long periods of time. The longevity of conference directors, then, is a clear advantage. Even with a number of new hires recently, the average tenure of conference directors is nearly a decade (9.25 years). In 2002, the "dean" of state Catholic conference directors was Gerald D'Avolio, who took over the Massachusetts Catholic Conference in 1975, not an insignificant fact for the political influence of the bishops in the state that was the epicenter of the scandal. In fact, D'Avolio's situation is instructive here. Over his three decades at the Massachusetts Catholic Conference, D'Avolio has known four Senate presidents and five House speakers, all of whom have been Catholic, respectful of the church, and receptive toward the church's political involvement. He has developed relationships with literally scores of legislators, relationships that would matter when the scandal erupted in Boston. D'Avolio recalls a particularly meaningful moment during the 2002 legislative session:

> There were many times in the heat of the *Globe* attack on His Eminence [Cardinal Law] and just prior to his resignation, during the constant, day-to-day badgering from the media, that I had to go up to the statehouse to try to impact public policy. After speaking up for so many years, you gain relationships, even with new or younger legislators coming in. So it was very heartening to me, for instance, standing in front of the Chamber of the Senate and having a number of senators come up to me while all this was going on and saying, "Gerry, I just want you to know that you convey a wonderful image up here, and we appreciate the fact that you are present here and speaking on some of the issues that are important to us and the citizens. We really appreciate you sticking it out here, and we encourage you to do more of it, even though we don't agree on everything." That made me feel very good. And that not only was conveyed by a number of senators, including the leadership, but on the House side, too.

Although D'Avolio represents the bishops of Massachusetts before the legislature, as a political advocate in the legislative arena he is not co-extensive with them. His boss might be known as "His Eminence," but to most legislators D'Avolio is simply "Gerry." Gerry was not the cause of the scandal in Boston, and consequently his relationships and credibility did not fall victim to it.[24]

Conference directors' experience and relationships are put into action in the practice of lobbying. Hollywood images of influence peddlers in Armani suits and Gucci loafers handing out money and favors to politicians aside, "the major currency lobbyists pedal today is information."[25] As society has grown more complex and the political responsibilities of state legislatures have increased, legislators rely more and more on interest groups to supply them with the information they need to make policy decisions.

Therefore, the credibility of interest groups is tied to the quality of information they supply. John Huebscher of the Wisconsin Catholic Conference suggests that this may be even more true for religious advocacy organizations than secular interest groups. "I think there is a temptation or tendency to view religious groups as idealistic do-gooders who don't understand the 'real world,' which is why being thoughtful and informed and being able to come in with data and analysis is so important to me—to quickly disabuse them of the idea that we don't know what we're talking about." Providing quality information to legislators is a vehicle for Catholic conferences to solidify their legitimacy as political actors in the eyes of legislators. As Huebscher puts it, "When I meet with a legislator, [the strategic objective] is to either establish or continue to cement their view of the Conference as an agency that provides thoughtful, useful information, so that even if they're disinclined to go with us on the issue of the moment, they will see in us someone that they would want to hear from again and that they would find it useful to hear from again because what we say would be thoughtful, informed, and helpful to them as they make a decision on an issue."

The centrality of information peddling in the legislative process suits state Catholic conferences well. Because they are not grassroots membership organizations, they do not rely heavily on mobilizing individuals to pressure legislators. As 501(c)(3) organizations, they cannot play the campaign finance and candidate endorsement game. Because information is their main currency, conference directors frequently tie their credibility to their reputations for "telling the truth." The experience of Robert O'Hara, the former utility lobbyist in Pennsylvania, is typical in this regard. "When I first started working for [the utility], I was told that the most important thing you've got up here is your credibility and don't ever lose it. The best way to maintain your credibility is to tell the truth. If you don't know it, say you don't know it; say you'll find out. That's been my approach." This is echoed by Vincent Senior, who led the Kentucky Catholic Conference from 2002 until his unexpected death in 2003 after a long career in government relations for business concerns. "If you get some false information to a legislator it will come back to haunt you," Senior warned. "You have to know your subject when you talk to them. A lot of times they'll say, 'Well, who's going to oppose this?' And you say, 'These groups: A, B, C.' 'Why would they oppose it?' And then you have to be able to tell them that. If you say, 'Nobody's going to oppose you, Senator, go ahead, you're free to do this,' and then suddenly someone does, you suffer." In his training to take over the Louisiana Catholic Conference, Daniel Loar quickly learned how to develop and maintain relationships with legislators. "Rule number one is never, never, *never* lie to a legislator. You're dead as a lobbyist if word gets around. Always tell the truth—always, always, *always*—even if the message you have to give is not one they want to hear." O'Hara summarizes the situation this way: "We're still only armed with a handshake and a smile around here. But credibility over time means more than just about anything, because people get to know you, and they don't expect that you're going to come in there and tell them something that's wrong. They may not agree with you, but they don't think you're going to lie to them. That's very important, and that helps them." Some bishops may be suspect in this respect in the wake of the scandal, but this does not directly impugn the reputation of state Catholic conference lobbyists like D'Avolio, Senior, Loar, Huebscher, and O'Hara.

Conceptualizing state conferences of Catholic bishops as dual structures helps us to see why the political influence of the bishops, working through the conferences, is not wholly dependent on the bishops' moral authority. That state Catholic conferences have bases of legitimacy independent of the bishops' moral authority does not mean that moral authority is irrelevant to their work, though. As Castagna of Oregon puts it, "What distinguishes the church's presence in the public policy arena is that it is based on the Gospels and the church's social teaching. Without that, I could be the lobbyist for the United Way." In concluding, then, I would like to suggest how the church's moral authority actually matters in specific public squares (as distinguished from the fictive *The* Public Square).

MORAL AUTHORITY REVISITED

Although they clearly have other political resources at their disposal, which they often use to good effect, when I ask state Catholic conference directors about the most important resource they possess in their political advocacy work, many look to the church's moral authority. O'Hara of Pennsylvania says, "The main thing is that the church has some moral authority. I mean, that's going in. I don't bring that to the job. It's there." Christopher Leifeld, executive director of the Minnesota Catholic Conference responds, "The bishops of Minnesota, our board, are looked to and respected as spiritual leaders, pastoral leaders, and voices of conscience, and I think that's our number one asset right there." I see two reasons the "Great Lenten Humiliation" of 2002 did not wholly evacuate the church's moral authority to speak in state legislative arenas.

Bishops, Not "the Bishops"

It is important to keep in mind the two dimensions of the scandal. There is the sexual abuse itself, and there is the episcopal malfeasance and mismanagement that perpetuated it. As research by the *New York Times* has documented, cases of sexual abuse have affected nearly every diocese.[26] But there is no evidence that the episcopal cover-up is as extensive. To the extent that there has been a loss of moral authority, it may more properly be said to apply to *bishops* and not *the* bishops. Many state Catholic conference directors express appreciation of the fact that their bishops have not been directly implicated in any misconduct. Although suspicion often seems to be cast over the entire church, in reality, the consequences of the scandal for bishops' moral authority in politics may be quite localized. After all, in former U.S. House speaker Tip O'Neill's well-worn phrase, "all politics is local."

Voice of the Tradition, Not the Bishops

Although state Catholic conferences are formally the public policy voice of their own states' bishops, they do not simply represent those particular men. As we saw in chapter 3, they represent the moral tradition of which those men are important teachers, a tradition that extends in space and time far beyond them. So, state Catholic conference staff are far more likely to invoke conciliar documents, like *Gaudium et Spes*, papal documents like *Evangelium Vitae*, U.S. bishops' documents like *Economic Justice for All*, and even the *Catechism of the Catholic Church*, than letters and statements produced by their own bishops. This practice reminds us that the church's tradition has a reality and force that is prior to and is only expressed by episcopal conferences. It is the voice of the tradition and not necessarily the voice of particular bishops that is heard in America's various public squares.

NOTES

An earlier and shorter version of this chapter appeared as "The Bishops and Politics" in *Commonweal*, 23 May 2003, pp. 17–20.

1. Boston Globe Spotlight Team, "Church Allowed Abuse by Priest for Years," *Boston Globe*, 6 January 2002, p. A1. See also The Investigative Staff of the *Boston Globe*, *Betrayal: The Crisis in the Catholic Church* (Boston: Little, Brown, 2002). This reporting earned the *Globe* a Pulitzer Prize. "*Annus horribilis*" is from an editorial by Paul Dinter, "A Catholic Crisis, Bestowed from Above," *New York Times*, 1 January 2003, p. A15. "Hideous truth" is from Daniel Johnson, "The Catholic Crisis," *Commentary*, February 2003, p. 26.

2. George Weigel, *The Courage to be Catholic: Crisis, Reform, and the Future of the Church* (New York: Basic Books, 2002), p. 1; Jay Dolan, *In Search of an American Catholicism: A History of Religion and Culture in Tension* (New York: Oxford University Press, 2002), p. 257.

3. Andrew Greeley, "Foreword to the Illinois Paperback Edition," in Jason Berry, *Lead Us Not into Temptation: Catholic Priests and the Sexual Abuse of Children* (Urbana, IL: University of Illinois Press, 2000), p. xx; Berry, *Lead Us Not Into Temptation*, p. xxii.

4. Peter Steinfels, *A People Adrift: The Crisis of the Roman Catholic Church in America* (New York: Simon & Schuster, 2003), p. 44.

5. Tom Beaudoin, "Our Catholic Watergate," *America*, 3–10 June 2002, p. 18; William Donohue, "The Catholic Church's Watergate," *beliefnet* interview by Deborah Caldwell, http://www.beliefnet.com/story/103/story_10367.html (accessed 29 January 2003).

6. I thank my colleague at the University of Virginia's Center on Religion and Democracy, Lara Diefenderfer, for offering this important cautionary note.

7. Seymour Martin Lipset and William Schneider, *The Confidence Gap: Business, Labor, and Government in the Public Mind* (New York: Free Press, 1983).

8. Larry Stammer, "Organized Religion Slips in Survey," *Los Angeles Times*, 11 January 2003, p. B18. It is perhaps worth noting that, even after its 15-point decline, confidence in organized religion is still twice that of confidence in "big business," which is consistently around 20 percent. See Catholic News Service graphic based on the Gallup Poll in *National Catholic Reporter*, 6 September 2002.

9. Jay Dolan, *In Search of an American Catholicism*, p. 258.

10. Rev. Bryan Hehir, "Leadership and Hope in a Time of Crisis and Conflict" (Catholic Charities USA membership meeting, Chicago, IL, 3 August 2002); Bishop William Skylstad quoted in *America* news briefs, 23 September 2002, p. 6.

11. Rev. Canice Connors quoted in "Bishops Question Grounds for War, Prelates Fear Scandal Drowning Out Voice," *Washington Post*, 15 November 2002, p. A2. *Times* quote from Robin Toner, "Testing the Church's Influence in Politics," *New York Times*, 26 January 2003, p. D2.

12. Arthur Jones, "Flood of New Abuse Cases Headed to California Courts," *National Catholic Reporter*, 23 January 2003; Tatsha Robertson, "Flood of Suits on Abuse Seen in California," *Boston Globe*, 1 January 2003, p. A1.

13. Public Act No. 02-138; Carrie Budoff and Alaine Griffin, "Stricter Molestation Law Approved by House," *Hartford Courant*, 9 May 2002, p. A9; Seth Stern, "More States Moving to Tighten Sex-Abuse Laws for Clergy," *Christian Science Monitor*, 10 June 2002; Thomas Szszkiewicz, "Suspicious Characters? Some Want Special Rules for Priests," *National Catholic Register*, 23 February–1 March 2003, p. 1.

14. Karen Ross, "Revealing Confidential Secrets: Will It Save Our Children?" *Seton Hall Law Review* 28 (1998): 963–999, quote from p. 964; C. Henry Kempe, Frederic N. Silverman, Brandt F. Steele, William Droegemuller, and Henry K. Silver, "The Battered Child Syndrome," *Journal of the American Medical Association* 181 (1962): 17–24; National Clearinghouse on Child Abuse and Neglect Information, *Current Trends in Child Maltreatment Reporting Laws* (Washington, DC: Department of Health and Human Services, 2002), p. 2.

15. In 1982, Missouri eliminated "minister" from its list of mandatory reporters. Mary Harter Mitchell, "Must Clergy Tell? Child Abuse Reporting Requirements Versus the Clergy Privilege and Free Exercise of Religion," *Minnesota Law Review* 71 (February 1987): 723–825.

16. *Reporting Laws: Mandatory Reporters of Child Abuse and Neglect* (Washington, DC: Department of Health and Human Services, 2002), p. 3.

17. Mitchell, "Must Clergy Tell?" pp. 735–36.

18. A possible exception would be 2003 New Hampshire House Bill 541, which included the following language: "A priest, rabbi, or ordained or licensed minister of any church or a duly accredited Christian Science practitioner shall not be required to disclose a confession or confidence made to him in his professional character as spiritual advisor, unless the person confessing or confiding waives the privilege. This section shall not apply to the disclosure of information relative to suspected or confirmed child abuse, and nothing in this section shall exempt a religious leader from RSA 169-C:29." But the last clause in this passage refers to the section of New Hampshire statute that already requires clergy to report suspected child abuse or neglect, and RSA 169-C:32 already specifically denies the clergy-penitent privilege in cases of child abuse or neglect. It is not clear, therefore, that this particular legislation changes the situation in New Hampshire at all.

19. "2003–2004 Legislative Session Lobbying Effort by Organization," Wisconsin State Ethics Board, http://ethics.state.wi.us/ (accessed 23 July 2003).

20. Ronald Hrebenar and Clive Thomas, "Interest Group Activity in the States," pp. 113–43 in Virginia Gray, Russell Hanson, and Herbert Jacob, eds., *Politics in the American States: A Comparative Analysis*, 7th ed. (Washington, DC: CQ Press, 1999).

21. Ronald Hedlund, "Wisconsin: Pressure Politics and a Lingering Progressive Tradition," pp. 305–44 in Ronald Hrebenar and Clive Thomas, eds., *Interest Group Politics in the Midwestern States* (Ames, IA: Iowa State University Press, 1993), p. 316. Contribution figure from Wisconsin Democracy Campaign, "2001–02 Committee Contributions to Candidates and LCCs," http://www.wisdc.org/WEB_PAC_Alpha2002.html (accessed 23 July 2003).

22. Also, its lobbying is limited to an "insubstantial part" of its activities, an amount specified nowhere but understood to be "something between 5 and 15 of the organization's total activities." Deirdre Dessingue, *Politics and the Pulpit: A Guide to the Internal Revenue Code Restrictions on the Political Activity of Religious Organizations* (Washington, DC: The Pew Forum on Religion and Public Life, 2002), p. 11.

23. Allen Hertzke, *Representing God in Washington: The Role of Religious Lobbies in the American Polity* (Knoxville, TN: University of Tennessee Press, 1988), pp. 69–70.

24. Which is not to say that the scandal had *no* political consequences in the Commonwealth of Massachusetts. See Michael Powell, "Catholic Clout is Eroded by Scandal," *Washington Post*, 6 July 2002, p. A1.

25. Dennis Dresang and James Gosling, *Politics and Policy in American States and Communities* (Boston: Allyn and Bacon, 1996), p. 160.

26. Laurie Goodstein, "Trail of Pain in Church Crisis Leads to Nearly Every Diocese," *New York Times*, 12 January 2003, p. A1.

5

Discourse

Liberally Clothing the Naked Public Square

John Huebscher's day begins early at his eleventh-floor office on Wilson Street, three blocks from the state capitol building in Madison, Wisconsin. Like many of his fellow legislative advocates—typically called, whether descriptively or derisively, "lobbyists"—he first checks for important faxes and e-mail ("action alerts") that may have come in over night from Washington, D.C. or Milwaukee. Finding nothing pressing, he scans the *New York Times*, pausing to enjoy a few escapist minutes with the crossword puzzle. He confers with his administrative assistant and two associates and then, on this particular morning, walks—efficiently and orderly, as befits his Swiss heritage—to his monthly breakfast meeting with Michael Blumenfeld and Sue Moline Larson, two other advocates who share some of his legislative concerns. They generously share ideas, information, and strategies over coffee and bagels at Ancora Coffee Roasters, one of Madison's many coffee shops. As the most experienced member of the group, Huebscher has more than his share of opportunities to offer commentary on the current legislative situation and prospects for the initiatives they favor. His colleagues listen intently as he makes predictions about the outcome of three or four bills currently pending, predictions that are borne out more often than not. They also discuss the advisability of issuing a joint statement on a bill that would adversely affect the organizations they represent.

When he returns to his office, Huebscher spends an increasing amount of time at his computer. For better or worse, the key written materials he relies on are now offered electronically. The Wheeler Report, a digest of the activities of the Wisconsin legislature that has been published since 1972, is available as an e-newsletter, which Huebscher reads. The many documents produced for the legislature each day, which were once printed and distributed through a document room, are now posted on the legislature's website. Huebscher mouses and scrolls his way through a score of newly introduced bills, committee hearing and floor session schedules, and the like. Although he has seen many of the bills before—some of them inevitably return, like bell-bottom pants—the cost of missing an important piece of legislation is high. So he carefully scans the seemingly endless stream of words on his computer monitor to see what kind of trouble the legislature is getting into. A large part of the morning staff meeting is dedicated to vetting the bills, assessing their likely future, and planning a strategy for engagement.

That strategy almost always entails explaining their position to the legislative or executive branch via letters and public testimony. So, later in the day, Huebscher and his associate Kathy Markeland head to the north wing of the capitol building. In an ornate hearing room, Huebscher appears before the Assembly Committee on Labor to offer testimony on a bill that would permit an employer "to refuse to employ, or to bar or terminate from employment, an individual who has been convicted of a felony." It is at this moment that we begin to see how he differs from the other lobbyists whose days in the capitol otherwise resemble his quite closely. Huebscher begins his testimony by declaring, "On behalf of the Wisconsin Catholic Conference, I am offering this testimony in opposition to Assembly Bill 353." He then outlines the basis for his opposition:

> Our stance on criminal justice issues is guided by the social teaching of the Catholic Church and insights gained from long experience ministering to prisoners, ex-offenders, crime victims, and their families. This experience guided development of the WCC's 1999 statement, *Public Safety, the Common Good, and the Church: A Statement on Crime and Punishment in Wisconsin.*
>
> The statement identifies several principles for evaluating public policies in the criminal justice area. Three of these principles that speak directly to issues raised in AB 353 are (1) that criminal justice policies serve the common good, (2) that they foster restoring victims and offenders to the community, and (3) that they exercise an option for the

poor and marginalized. On this latter point, policies must be assessed in light of their impact on racial minorities.

Of course, Huebscher was not the only lobbyist to appear before the assembly committee in opposition to this "felon bias" bill. But he was unique in grounding his opposition in *religious* authority and ideas, principally "the social teaching of the Catholic Church" manifested in a statement issued by Wisconsin's Roman Catholic bishops.

Huebscher—like his colleagues Michael Blumenfeld and Sue Larson—is a *religious lobbyist*. Indeed, he is the dean of religious lobbyists in Madison, having worked for the Wisconsin Catholic Conference since 1987 and served as its executive director since 1992. According to the Wisconsin Catholic Conference's literature, "With the message of the Gospel and the social teachings of the church as its foundation, the WCC offers a specifically Catholic contribution to state and federal public policy debates." How exactly that Catholic contribution to public policy debates manifests itself, in Wisconsin and nationally, is the question this chapter answers through an analysis of public testimony given by state Catholic conferences.

RELIGIOUS ARGUMENTS IN THE NAKED PUBLIC SQUARE

In the 1980s, Richard John Neuhaus famously characterized the American public square as "naked." The metaphor of the naked public square captured his view that our contemporary "political doctrine and practice . . . exclude religion and religiously grounded values from the conduct of public business."[1] While this view had great resonance with many, it also seemed to ignore the various ways in which religious voices have played and continue to play a prominent role in American public life. We need not look back to the abolitionist and temperance movements, or even to the more recent civil rights and peace movements, to find robust examples of religious participation in American public life. In fact, at the very time Neuhaus was proclaiming the public square religiously naked, Americans United for Separation of Church and State was warning that the "New Christian Right" was threatening to break down the wall of separation between church and state.[2]

Religious voices are certainly present in American's various public squares. This does not mean, however, that Neuhaus has completely misunderstood the situation. To the contrary, there is a sense in which the naked public square captures a basic sociological fact: the modern polity is fundamentally secular. In this sense, "secularization" is a constitutive element of our modern institutions. In Jose Casanova's excellent summary, "the core and central thesis of the theory of secularization is the conceptualization of the process of societal modernization as a process of institutional differentiation and emancipation of secular spheres—primarily the state, the economy, and science—from the religious sphere." Consequently, "the primary 'public' institutions (state, economy) no longer need or are interested in maintaining a sacred cosmos or a public religious worldview."[3] Thus, the naked public square is a reality of modern society.

But for some, particularly academic political philosophers, it is not sufficient that the polity be constitutionally secular. They also want to place restrictions on the appearance or use of religious convictions in the public sphere. The question of the naked public square at this second level becomes this: what role should religiously grounded morality play in liberal democratic political deliberation?[4] The question is a normative one: Should religious arguments (or "reasons") be excluded from public debate? If not, should those motivated by their religious convictions exercise self-restraint in presenting their views in public?

Other than Richard Rorty, who sees "religion as a conversation-stopper," few serious political philosophers today would exclude religious arguments entirely from the public square.[5] So the first question is largely settled in the *negative*: religious reasons should not be entirely excluded from public debate. What Paul Weithman calls the "standard approach" to citizenship in liberal democracy, however, answers the second question in the *affirmative*. According to this version of liberalism—associated most especially with John Rawls, but also with Robert Audi, Charles Larmore, Amy Guttman, and others—good citizenship demands willingness to participate in public debate in the right way. Because religious reasons are not accessible to all citizens, they are divisive and undemocratic, and so they must be "made good" by appeal to ones that are accessible.[6]

Christopher Eberle calls this standard approach *justificatory liberalism* for its emphasis on appropriate *public justifications* in liberal politics. Justificatory liberals' "doctrine of restraint" suggests that a citizen "ought to withhold support for any coercive law for which he can't discern a public justification." Because an appropriate public justification is one which "articulates in some appropriate way with the distinctive and divergent points of view of [a citizen's] compatriots," religious reasons are excluded by definition as public justifications. In fact, in this view, religious reasons are the *"paradigmatic* example of a nonpublic, or *personal,* justification."[7]

A growing number of political philosophers, including well-known liberals like Michael Perry, are questioning the "exclusionist" position represented by the standard approach.[8] Among the challenges they issue is the question of whether religiously grounded arguments are any less "publicly accessible" or any less divisive than other, secular arguments.[9] In the United States particularly, religiously based arguments could be *more* accessible, given the high rates of religiosity found in this country. As Michael Perry has argued, echoing Stephen Carter's earlier sentiment, "certain basic moral premises common to the Jewish and Christian traditions, in conjunction with the supporting religious premises, still constitute the fundamental moral horizon of most Americans—much more than do Kantian (or neo-Kantian) premises, or Millsian premises, or Nietzschean premises (and so forth)."[10]

Furthermore, even if not all religious people *agree* in their beliefs, it does not mean that arguments based on scripture, for example, are not comprehensible to a wide spectrum of the population. Of course not everyone will agree with every particular interpretation of scripture, but neither will everyone agree with every particular reading of economic trend data. As Jeffrey Stout argues, there is no "moral Esperanto"[11]—hence the necessity of politics.[12]

Thus, scholars such as Eberle, Perry, Weithman, and Nicholas Wolterstorff reject the doctrine of restraint in its pure form. However, according to Eberle, "even if religious citizens have no moral obligation to adhere to the doctrine of restraint, they're still morally obliged to obey the ideal of conscientious engagement."[13] That is, those who would bring their religious convictions to bear on public life need to do so responsibly and conscientiously out of respect for their fellow citizens. A version of this view can be found in one of Weithman's two principal claims in *Religion and the Obligations of Citizenship*:

> Citizens of a liberal democracy may offer arguments in public political debate which depend upon reasons drawn from their comprehensive

moral views, including their religious views, without making them good by appeal to other arguments—provided they believe that their government would be justified in adopting the measures they favor and are prepared to indicate what they think would justify the adoption of the measures.[14]

Eberle himself summarizes this spirit even more succinctly in his core thesis: "a citizen is morally permitted to support (or oppose) a coercive law even if he has only a religious rationale for that law." But, "each citizen ought sincerely and conscientiously to attempt to articulate a plausible, secular rationale for any coercive law she supports."[15]

As we will see, this view is not only good political philosophy, but is reflective of the sociological reality of politics as well. Although there is nothing about liberal democracy that *requires* secular reasons, there is much about a secular political institution that *compels* them.

PRODUCING THE SACRED IN THE PUBLIC SQUARE

In *The Restructuring of American Religion* and again in *Producing the Sacred*, the sociologist Robert Wuthnow points to the growth and increasing importance on the American scene of religious special purpose or special interest groups. According to his analysis of the *Encyclopedia of Organizations*, in 1985 there were some 800 nationally incorporated religious special purpose groups. "Since 1960," Wuthnow reports, "approximately 300 new organizations have been founded. And since World War II the number of new organizations totals nearly 500. This means, of course, that the majority of special purpose groups in American religion . . . is far larger than at any time in American history. At the close of the Civil War, for example, no more than several dozen such groups were known to have been in existence." The implications of this growth in religious special purpose groups are significant, especially for those groups whose main concern is some aspect of "public affairs."[16]

According to Wuthnow, the way groups "produce the sacred" in public arenas is shaped by the socio-cultural environment in which the groups exist. While he recognizes the constraining aspects of the secular socio-cultural environment that characterizes contemporary America, Wuthnow is also sensitive to the enabling aspects. His elaboration of this subtle position merits being quoted at length.

Religious special interest groups need to be understood in relation to the wider environmental resources and constituencies that make them possible in the first place and that influence their contribution to the public expression of religious values. Among these conditions it is especially important to consider the relationship between religious special interest groups and the secular emphasis of contemporary society, the growing role of the state, and the highly rationalized character of modern institutions. . . . The relationship between religious special interest groups and their environment is thus a symbiotic one. For their part, these groups are able to flourish because the broader environment is already heavily laden with such groups. But the rationalized and formally organized character of the social environment, in turn, is reinforced by the fact that religious special interest groups conform so closely to its procedures.

Wuthnow concludes that no religious organization "is prevented from producing expressions of the sacred that can be communicated in the public arena, but all of them are constrained to speak in certain languages and to say some things rather than others."[17] And here he doesn't mean they are normatively constrained but that they are constrained by the way modern social institutions actually function.

Allen Hertzke's landmark work on religious lobbying provides an excellent example of how this looks in a particular political institution at a particular moment in time. In *Representing God in Washington*, Hertzke provides one of the few scholarly studies to date of religious lobbies in Washington, D.C. He notes that in 1950 there were 16 major religious lobbies in D.C., and by 1985, there were at least 80.[18] This religious special interest group explosion coincides with the advocacy explosion in general, both being driven by the expansion of the state into ever more areas of life. In this sense, already suggested by Wuthnow above, the expansion of the secular state enables the numeric growth of religious advocacy organizations in the political sphere. But, again, these groups must accept, in large part, the secular "rules" of the political "game," especially if they have any serious intention of realizing concrete political victories.[19]

Of particular interest here is one major case Hertzke highlights in which religious lobbies were effective in realizing their goal: the Equal Access Act of 1984. As Hertzke summarizes it, "The Act stipulates that it is illegal for a school district that grants the use of school facilities to voluntary extracurricular student groups before or after school to deny the same use to student-initiated groups on the basis of 'religious, political, philosophical, or other content of the speech at such meetings.'" What is interesting in terms of this analysis is that, in lobbying for this act, fundamentalist religious groups came to "embrace the language of rights," which "is more appealing than the language of moral imperatives" in the congressional context. As a Moral Majority lobbyist told Hertzke, "We can't afford to say 'God settled it, that's it.'" The Moral Majority learned from the success of "rights talk" over "God talk" in the Equal Access Act, and would attempt to apply it to other issues in which they were involved. To wit, Jerry Falwell has said, speaking of the abortion issue in particular, "We are reframing the debate. This is no longer a religious issue, but a civil rights issue." From this example it seems clear that the congressional milieu shapes and constrains religious groups that seek to influence Congress. Groups proliferate, but religious rhetoric "inevitably seems to give way to lobby strategies aimed at change on the margins."[20] Hertzke found plenty of evidence for the fact that the norms and priorities of the political institution itself "mold the message" of religious groups seeking to influence the political institution.

In the end, any group that wants to be taken seriously in the public square comes to present their arguments in ways that are persuasive to people who act on motivations that may include religious ones but also other ideas and ideals, such as the need to represent one's constituency and be re-elected, the need to raise money and keep donors happy, ideas advanced by competing interest groups, and ethical beliefs beyond those that are prescribed by religion.

To be sure, some will not do this. But more mature religious advocacy organizations will. We saw this in the evolution of the Christian Right in its heyday on Capitol Hill. We see it in the recent political advocacy of Mainline Protestants in Washington.[21] And I expect to see it among state Catholic conferences as well. After all, the organizations are over three decades old, on average. Moreover, the average tenure of current executive directors is almost a decade, and the modal executive director today comes out of a state government background. They know how the political game works, and bishops hire them explicitly because they know how the game works. The balance of this chapter, then, is given over to an empirical examination of state Catholic conferences' approaches to publicly arguing for their preferred policy positions. Specifically, I focus on public arguments presented in legislative testimony.

ANALYZING TESTIMONY

Testifying at legislative hearings is both one of the most prevalent and one of the most important activities of political advocacy organizations. According to Kay Schlozman and John Tierney's authoritative study, testifying at hearings is the most common technique for influencing public policy employed by political organizations in Washington, D.C. Fully *99 percent* of organizations in their study reported using the tactic. This is true also of religious advocacy organizations in the nation's capital, though slightly less so than for the organizational population. Daniel Hofrenning found that 91 percent of religious lobbyists he surveyed reported testifying at hearings as a tactic their organization used to influence policy. These same high levels obtain in the statehouses as well, where Anthony Nownes and Patricia Freeman found that 99 percent of political organizations offer public testimony.[22] One hundred percent of state Catholic conferences report testifying at legislative hearings (see table 4.2).

The empirical material for this chapter is recent legislative testimony given by state Catholic conferences on four issues central to their political advocacy and to the controversies surrounding religion and public life: (1) abortion, (2) criminal justice (especially the death penalty), (3) same sex marriage, and (4) economic justice (especially welfare).[23] I examine the place of religion in the public policy argumentation of state Catholic conferences by content analyzing this testimony. Specifically, I explore the extent to which religious groups employ *specifically religious legitimations* in their public testimony, compared to broader *cultural legitimations*. Building on the work of sociologist Michele Dillon, I identify six categories of religious legitimation and six categories of cultural legitimation.[24] Table 5.1 gives a descriptive overview of these coding categories, including a representative example of each type of legitimation, and the frequency with which they were invoked in the total sample.[25]

That state Catholic conferences do not rely exclusively, or even predominantly, on religious arguments can be seen in the overall distribution of arguments in table 5.1. In fact, a minority of the legitimations in the testimony were religious (37.6 percent), while 23.2 percent were "civil religious," and 39.3 percent were secular.

Table 5.2 examines the legitimations offered by issue area. Here some interesting differences emerge. First of all, on criminal justice is-

Table 5.1. Legitimations Presented by State Catholic Conferences in Testimony before State Legislatures

Type	Example	% of Total
Religious Legitimations		
Scripture	"God decrees in his law that you shall not murder, and in this Commandment God forbids the taking away of our life or the lives of others unjustly."	1.6
Church Tradition & Teaching	"The Church's teaching on the matter is clear—abortion is never permissible."	14.5
Church Documents	"The *Catechism of the Catholic Church* teaches that the psychological genesis of homosexuality remains largely unexplained."	4.3
Church Leaders	"The Holy Father urges us to ensure proper support for families and motherhood."	11.8
Personal Authority	"As a religious leader, I find this bill a distressing and offensive measure."	3.8
Other	"I believe that there are some absolutes. In my case, from God."	1.6
Total		37.6
Cultural Legitimations		
CIVIL RELIGIOUS LEGITIMATIONS		
Law & Morality	"Respect for marriage is not the imposition of one sectarian dogma but the recognition by people of many faiths of what Jefferson called a 'self-evident truth' in the natural law."	21.0
National/State Identity	"Such a commitment will also reflect a social vision more compatible with the progressive and humane tradition of the state."	2.2
Total		23.2

SECULAR LEGITIMATIONS	
Scientific Authority	"According to Dr. Frank Boehm, a self-proclaimed pro-choice physician and Director of Vanderbilt U. Medical Center, 'Never is a partial birth abortion needed or indicated.'"	7.0
Legal Authority	"The U.S. Supreme Court declared in 1885 that any prospective state had to have laws resting on 'the basis of the idea of the family, as consisting in and springing from the union for life of one man and one woman in the holy estate of matrimony.'"	19.9
Socioeconomic Analysis	"Numerous studies show that marriage itself is a societal good. Typical is a study in the *American Journal of Sociology* that finds married couples have longer lifespans than unmarried people."	11.3
Personal Experience	"I doubt [that homosexual people will become straight] because I myself spent several years emotionalof my own life trying just exactly that, finding myself unsuccessful, and creating an wake for myself and others."	1.1
Total		39.3

Note: Based on analysis of 186 legitimations in 54 pieces of testimony by 21 conferences.

Table 5.2.   Legitimations Presented by State Catholic Conferences by Issue Area

Type	Abortion	Criminal Justice	Same Sex Marriage	Economic Justice
Religious Legitimations				
Scripture	0%	2.8%	2.8%	2.8%
Church Tradition				
& Teaching	14.0	19.4	19.4	8.8
Church Documents	1.8	11.1	0	5.3
Church Leaders	5.3	30.6	5.6	10.5
Personal Authority	0	2.8	8.3	5.3
Other	0	2.8	2.8	1.8
Total	21.1	69.5	38.9	34.5
Cultural Legitimations				
Civil Religious Legitimations				
Law & Morality	28.1%	8.3%	27.8%	17.5%
National/State Identity	5.3	0	0	1.8
Total	33.4	8.3	27.8	19.3
Secular Legitimations				
Scientific Authority	14.0%	2.8%	0%	7.0%
Legal Authority	26.3	16.7	30.6	8.8
Socioeconomic				
Analysis	5.3	0	2.8	29.8
Personal Experience	0	2.8	0	1.8
Total	45.6	22.3	33.4	47.4
Totals	100	100	100	100

Note: Based on analysis of 186 legitimations in 54 pieces of testimony by 21 conferences.

sues, religious legitimations are dominant (69.5 percent). In particular, references to "church teaching and tradition" (19.4 percent) and to "church leaders" (30.6 percent) were common. This is due largely to testimony on the death penalty that pointed to the development of the church's teaching on the immorality of the death penalty in contemporary society, especially Pope John Paul II's leadership in advancing this teaching. This is evident in the Nebraska Catholic Conference's testimony in support of legislation that would abolish the death penalty. In his March 2003 testimony before the legislature's Judiciary Committee, Executive Director James Cunningham argued that "application of [the Catholic Church's] teaching regarding the death penalty has become clearer in recent years; a new understanding has evolved.

Much of this is due to the clear and energetic teaching efforts of Pope John Paul II. In his great and important encyclical, *The Gospel of Life*, the Pope formulated a standard for application of this teaching, a test for the death penalty if you will. That test is this: is the death penalty *absolutely necessary*; that is, are there no other means left to defend against aggressors, preserve public order and protect the safety of individuals and families? In his role as head of the Church worldwide, the Pope himself responds that the cases of absolute necessity are extremely rare if not practically nonexistent.

When Governor Tim Pawlenty proposed reinstating the death penalty in Minnesota, the Minnesota Catholic Conference observed in its February 2004 testimony before the House Judiciary Policy and Finance Committee, "Pope John Paul II, in his visit to St. Louis, Missouri, in 1999, pleaded with the governor of Missouri not to impose the death penalty on the convict Darrell Mease. He has stated clearly that the moral conditions for the use of capital punishment no longer exist in our present day society." Similarly, in testimony opposing the expansion of the definition of capital murder as a defense against terrorism, the Kansas Catholic Conference notes, "While visiting St. Louis in 1999, Pope John Paul II called capital punishment 'cruel and unnecessary' to keep society safe."

On same sex marriage, a plurality of the arguments are religious (38.9 percent), but the single most common argument given by the church has to do with legal authority (30.6 percent). This is especially clear in the testimony of the New Jersey Catholic Conference in support of a bill that would prohibit same sex marriage. Executive Director William Bolan, an attorney by training, begins his testimony before the Senate Judiciary Committee by putting the issue in its legal context.

Before addressing the substantive issue it is important to understand the legal context in which this bill has been introduced. . . . Under the Full Faith and Credit Clause, the public acts, records and judicial proceedings of every other state are entitled to recognition in other states unless extension of those rights and benefits would be illegal, violate fundamental public policy or allow citizens purposefully to evade legal restrictions in their own states. But the Full Faith and Credit Clause does not require a state to act contrary to its own public policy, and thus the constitutional question turns on whether there is a state policy in favor of heterosexual marriages and in opposition to same sex unions.

In *M.T. v. J.T.*, 140 N.J. Super. 77, 84 (App. Div. 1976), certif. Den. 71 N.J. 345 (1976) the court held that a lawful marriage requires performance of a ceremonial marriage of two persons of the opposite sex, a male and female. Referring to our marriage statute *N.J.S.A.* 37:1-1 *eq seq.*, the court noted that our marriage statute does not contain an explicit reference to a requirement that the marriage must be between a man and woman, but the statutory condition is so "strongly and firmly implied from a full reading of the statute that a different legislative intent, one which would sanction a marriage between persons of the same sex, cannot be fathomed." Thus, it is important that state policy be clear in its favoring of heterosexual marriages so as to defeat a finding that New Jersey must give full faith and credit to a Hawaii marriage of a homosexual couple.

Similar legal argumentation is used by Dick Dowling of Maryland (who is also an attorney): "It is settled that 'the law in this State only contemplates and authorizes a "marriage" between a man and a woman.' Attorney General Francis Burch said that in a 1972 opinion which also says this: '. . . in the present state of the law, it is perfectly clear that sameness of sex of the parties constitutes a legal impediment to marriage. . . .'" There is obviously a recognition that the courts are a key battleground on which the issue of same sex marriage will be fought.

In the other two issue areas, cultural legitimations predominate, though there is variation in which type of cultural legitimation is most common. Secular argumentation is most common overall on abortion (45.6 percent), though the single most common legitimation offered by state Catholic conferences in the abortion area is civil religious. Of the arguments coded, 28.1 percent were on "law and morality." On the abortion issue, the conferences most typically connect the law of the land to non-specifically religious moral ideals (the dignity of the person, human rights, the common good), ideals that emerge from the church's understanding of the natural law. For example, the Michigan Catholic Conference's testimony on the "Legal Birth Definition Act" includes the following argument: "The sanctity and dignity of human life is the cornerstone of Catholic moral reflection and social teaching and at the heart of the Church's public policy agenda. Human dignity stands at the heart of every issue we speak to. . . . Surely, no reasonable person could disagree, that the state has a compelling interest in protecting the life of a born person." The Nebraska Catholic Conference argues for an informed consent law on abortion by declaring that "it is the proper role of government to safeguard and support all human life, not to facilitate, or be ambivalent toward, its destruction.

This bill is not only a legitimate and good expression of government's proper role, it is the right thing for a caring society to do." A "Choose Life" license plate, according to the Ohio Catholic Conference, "incorporates a message that we believe is consistent with our nation's founding ideals to protect life, liberty and the pursuit of happiness."

Some conferences also tied their positions to the fundamental identity of the United States as a nation. In the 2001–2002 session, legislation was introduced in Kansas to create a "health care providers' right of conscience." This right of conscience would allow health care service providers (individuals, institutions, or payers) to refuse to participate in or pay for health care services that they find morally objectionable. House Bill 2711 included the following definition: "'Health care services subject to this act' means any health care service relating to abortion, artificial insemination, assisted reproduction, artificial birth control prescribed for a contraceptive purpose, human cloning, embryonic stem cell and fetal experimentation, infanticide, assisting suicide, euthanasia, and sterilization for contraceptive purposes." Mike Farmer, executive director of the Kansas Catholic Conference, provided testimony to the Senate Public Health and Welfare Committee on behalf of the bishops. Among his arguments in support of the bill was that

> *forcing* people and institutions to violate the convictions of their conscience is a characteristic of an entirely different form of government than ours. To trample upon the demands of conscience is far removed from the ideals that are at the heart of the American experiment. Respect for diversity of conscience is a core value for all Kansans and all Americans. Protection and respect for rights of conscience has been a centerpiece of American law from our Nation's founding; it is a value long enshrined in our National and State constitutions. To reject this foundational value now is to ignore, and ultimately to extinguish, an essential liberty, a liberty that led to our Nation's founding and for which men and women have sacrificed their lives.

To the pro-choice movement's emphasis on the constitutional right to privacy, state Catholic conferences like Kansas pose the constitutional right of conscience.

On economic justice issues, secular argumentation predominates (47.4 percent), and the primary legitimation invoked by state Catholic conferences is socioeconomic analysis (29.8 percent). Legislation that bears on questions of economic justice (e.g., welfare, living wage, health care access) can be highly technical, and many (Catholics included) have criticized the bishops' conferences for engaging in public policy debate in an issue area in which the bishops lack expertise. But while the bishops themselves lack expertise to engage economic policy issues, their staff are able to draw on the expertise of others, just as most other interest groups do. For example, in a February 2000 statement in support of a Predatory Home Loan Act, the Illinois Catholic Conference argues,

> Clearly, as a society, we should protect an individual's ability to maintain their primary place of residence. Yet, despite the healthy economy, statistics indicate that the number of sub/prime loan foreclosures in Illinois has been rapidly increasing in recent years. One reason for the increase is due to the practice known as "predatory lending." Predatory lending occurs when unscrupulous lenders or brokers target those who are "equity-rich," but "cash poor" by charging excessive points or fees. HB 3007 would limit the amount lenders and brokers may charge for fees and points to an amount that cannot exceed three percent of the loan value. Given the average for loans and fees is generally 1.5 percent, we feel that this cap is a reasonable limit to place on lenders and brokers.

Similarly, testimony of the Maryland Catholic Conference on the "Welfare Innovation Act of 2000" notes, "In our state, over 225,000 households live at or below 150 percent of the federal poverty level. Many of these families are transitioning from welfare to work. In this endeavor, they are finding it challenging, difficult, and in some cases outright impossible to keep up with their food, housing, health care, child care and transportation expenses while earning low hourly wages (an average of $6.43 per hour for those leaving welfare)."

In one unique but telling case from 2002, the Michigan Catholic Conference went so far as to commission a study of the earned income tax credit (EITC) by Anderson Economic Group, an economics and public policy consulting group in Lansing.[26] To facilitate additional financial relief for the working poor, the Michigan Catholic Conference for several years had advocated a state EITC to complement the federal EITC—to no avail. As vice president for public policy Paul Long describes the situation, a Michigan EITC had received support in the past from Democrats, but Republicans remained unconvinced.

It was our belief that in order to advance the debate on this issue we needed to have a credible, sound research document that looked at the issue and provided recommendations to state policy makers. So we commissioned Patrick Anderson. Patrick is a well-known and very credible conservative economist here in Michigan. We felt that having him as the author of the report would gives us—just from a purely political perspective—entrée to the folks that we've had trouble gaining support from. . . . While the EITC has received support nationally from Republicans, here in Michigan it was kind of like banging your head up against a wall. So we commissioned the report as an effort to give us some traction and move it forward.

Although the report did not mechanically lead to the creation of an EITC in Michigan, it did give the Michigan Catholic Conference an additional set of arguments to use in their effort to persuade legislators that an EITC "would be good public policy for the people of Michigan."[27]

Combining Religious and Secular Arguments

That state Catholic conferences combine different legitimations in their testimony is already hinted at by the fact that 186 legitimations were coded from 54 pieces of testimony, an average of 3.4 legitimations per testimony. Table 5.3 shows the patterns of arguments found in the content analysis.

In only 11.1 percent of the cases do conferences offer *exclusively religious* legitimations—though this figure is inflated by the extensive use of exclusively religious arguments on criminal justice (for reasons

Table 5.3. Pattern of Argumentation in Public Hearings (Overall and by Issue Area)

Pattern	Overall	Abortion	Criminal Justice	Same Sex Marriage	Economic Justice
Religious Only	11.1%	7%	36%	8%	0%
Civil Religious Only	1.9	0	0	8	0
Secular Only	7.4	0	0	8	18
Religious and Civil Religious	9.3	7	9	17	6
Religious and Secular	18.5	0	36	17	23.5
Civil Religious and Secular	18.5	40	0	8	18
Religious, Civil Religious, and Secular	35.2	47	18	33	35
Total	100	100	100	100	100
	(n=54)	(n=15)	(n=11)	(n=12)	(n=17)

Note: Columns may not total exactly 100% due to rounding.

highlighted already). On economic justice, state Catholic conferences never use only religious arguments, and on abortion and same sex marriage they do so only 7 and 8 percent of the time, respectively. Overall, the most common pattern found in state Catholic conference testimony is a combination of religious, civil religious, and secular arguments (35.2 percent of all testimony).

A good example of this is the testimony of Marlene Lao-Collins, associate director of social concerns at the New Jersey Catholic Conference, on a new "standard of need" proposed by the state's Department of Human Services. Lao-Collins's statement in its entirety is included as an appendix to this chapter. It includes reference to "the Church's belief that each individual possesses an inherent dignity and priceless worth because he or she is created in the image of God" (religious argument). It also makes reference to human rights and the responsibility of society to protect them (civil religious argument). And it gives over the most space to empirical observations and data about the state of the poor: observations drawn from Catholic programs and institutions caring for the needy, from poverty statistics, and from a study of the cost of living in New Jersey by a Dr. Diana Pearce (secular arguments).

Although the New Jersey Catholic Conference grounds it position on the standard of need in a religious view of human dignity, simply asserting that view is not a sufficient argument in the legislative arena. Like so many other state Catholic conferences, it frequently bundles its religious arguments with civil religious and/or secular arguments. In their various attempts to persuade legislators through public testimony, state Catholic conferences cast a wide argumentative net.

Roma Locuta Est, Causa Finita Est?

This wide argumentative net ought to be reassuring to those who fear that religious speech in the public square is divisive. It also invites a reconsideration of Richard Rorty's and other liberals' concern about the invocation of religion in public deliberation as a "conversation-stopper." Recently, Rorty has amended his argument to say that "neither law nor custom should stop [people] from bringing [their] favorite texts with [them] into the public square." Whether that text is Psalm 72, which Nicholas Wolterstorff prefers, or Mill's *On Liberty*, which Rorty prefers, does not matter. Either one could serve as a conversation starter or conversation stopper; they have the same epistemological status. What Rorty continues to maintain, then, is that "religious believers should not justify their support of or opposition to legislation *simply* by saying 'Scripture says' or 'Rome has spoken; the matter is closed' or 'My church teaches. . . .' It is one thing to explain how a given political stance is bound up with one's religious beliefs, and another to think that it is enough, when defending a political view, simply to cite authority, scriptural or otherwise." In brief, "What should be discouraged is *mere* appeal to authority."[28]

There is no doubt that some religious persons make political arguments merely by appeal to religious authority. But in actually existing public squares—like a legislative hearing room—these arguments are not taken seriously. So professional religious advocates avoid them. Even when Rome is invoked in testimony, state Catholic conferences do not pretend "the matter is closed." For example, the Nevada Catholic Conference begins its testimony on the death penalty by "affirming the position of Pope John Paul II and the United States Conference of Catholic Bishops." But the testimony later acknowledges, "We realize there are many in our own society including active members of our faith who hold contrary views" (to those of the Pope and the bishops). And, significantly, it concludes, "We know that each of you will carefully consider the serious nature of the issue and direct Nevada on the right path." Not only does this testimony not merely appeal to authority, it relativizes the authority of the bishops.

As Richard Fenn has argued in his analysis of the secularization of religious language, "In secular contexts, even individuals with strong religious convictions find that they are expected to engage in a version of 'seminar talk': to advance personal opinions or to make suggestions rather than to proclaim or declare. When religious witness does occur, moreover, constraints are imposed on the witness's ability to exhort and direct, let alone to declare, pronounce, and to judge. These more authoritative speech-acts are reserved in secular contexts to those licensed to speak with authority."[29] Legislators can direct, religious advocates can only plead. So, analysis of state Catholic conference testimony reveals frequent use of language such as "please partner with us," "please consider," "we ask," "we encourage," "we hope," and "we respectfully request." The strongest and most common language used in testimony by state Catholic conferences is "urge," as in "We urge a Do Pass recommendation on this bill" (North Dakota) or "We urge the advancement of LB 791 to General File" (Nebraska). But this language does more to convey the sense of urgency conferences bring to the legislation than to suggest that they have any authority to bring closure to the matter by virtue of having spoken. Richard Rorty harbors the Enlightenment desire for ecclesiastical organizations to die off, but he and other political liberals certainly cannot have any principled objection to this sort of public speech by religious advocacy organizations.

CONCLUSION

In the end, when state Catholic conferences engage in political debate, they are "liberally clothing the naked public square." They recognize and must accommodate themselves to the pluralistic, secular public square in which they operate—hence the frequency of civil religious and secular arguments, as well as combinations of different types of arguments, seen in the testimony analyses in this chapter. But the idea of removing religious arguments entirely from their testimony is so foreign to the staff of state Catholic conferences that when I asked about this in interviews I was met with confusion. The question itself did not even make sense. The situation was reminiscent of the scenario constructed by law professor Steven D. Smith in an article about religion in the public square: "Asking whether citizens should be permitted to rely on religious convictions in addressing moral issues will seem to the devout a bit like asking whether horses should be allowed to run in the Kentucky Derby, or whether participation in symphony orchestras should be open to musicians. The questions seem a bit peculiar, but I suppose the appropriate response is still to smile and say 'yes.'"[30]

CHAPTER 5 APPENDIX: STATEMENT OF THE NEW JERSEY CATHOLIC CONFERENCE IN CONNECTION WITH PUBLIC HEARINGS ON STANDARD OF NEED

Department of Human Services
March 4, 2002

The New Jersey Catholic Conference appreciates the opportunity to comment on the Department of Human Services proposed new rule for the "Standard of Need" issued in the New Jersey Register on January 7, 2002. We would also like to compliment the Department of Human Services for its commitment to adjusting the "standard of need."

The New Jersey Catholic Conference will propose three recommendations we believe are essential to ensuring a complete and accurate "standard of need" is established and upheld. We recommend 1.) inclusion of other items such as utilities, child-care and health care in your calculations, 2.) the self-sufficiency standard be used to determine cost and 3.) that the Department pursue setting cash benefits at the level of the "standard of need" established.

The Church brings to the table broad experience in serving those in need. The Catholic community through its numerous programs and institutions educates the young, cares for the sick, shelters the homeless, feeds the hungry, assists needy families, welcomes refugees, and serves the elderly. It is through this vast experience that we are able to see first hand the devastating impact of poverty on families and children.

The effects of New Jersey's current public assistant levels on human lives are staggering. Families and individuals are often forced to seek food from family and friends, food pantries, soup kitchens—or they do without. Catholic Charities emergencies services located throughout the state provide families with assistance in food, rent and utilities. Recently they reported to the New Jersey Catholic Conference that in the last year before September 11, 2001 and the realities of an economic downturn including budget deficit, they were seeing disturbing increases in the number of families seeking assistance. They also noted that many more return frequently and a substantially increasing number are working poor.

Considering that New Jersey is one of the wealthiest states in the nation it was troubling when the Catholic Campaign for Human Development's report "Poverty USA: America's Forgotten State" revealed that of the 10 top poorest cities in the United States with a population of over 250,000, Newark ranks 4th with 26.5 percent of the people living below the poverty line. Emergency service providers in that region reported that, unlike other parts of the state, the majority of families served in Newark were on public assistance. In every case, working poor or on public assistance, families are simply unable to provide even the basic necessities like housing, food and clothing making it increasingly difficult to maintain healthy and sustainable lives for themselves and their children.

The New Jersey Catholic Bishops believe that expecting families to live in abject poverty while on public assistance or at low wages is a fundamentally moral issue. The right to a sufficient amount of food, to decent, affordable housing and health care are among the most important of human rights. These rights are grounded in the Church's belief that each individual possesses an inherent dignity and priceless worth because he or she is created in the image of God. It is the responsibility of society to protect such. We cannot continue to permit the human dignity of so many families and individuals dependent on cash assistance or other benefits to be undermined.

In 1989 [the] Supreme Court of New Jersey ruled that "the 'standard of need' is the amount of money which has been determined to be essential to maintain an acceptable standard of living." The statutory definition as cited in N.J.S.A. 44:10–34 defines the "standard of need" as the *minimum amount of income and in-kind benefits or services needed* by families and single persons living in New Jersey in order *to maintain a decent and healthy standard of living*, as established by regulation of the Commissioner, and shall include necessary items such as housing, utilities, food, work-related transportation, clothing, and personal household essentials.

To meet this mandate it is necessary to identify those components needed to *maintain a decent and healthy standard of living* as well as determine an adequate method of calculating the amount needed by a family or single adult to sufficiently meet its basic needs. In regards to the latter, given the process of moving families from welfare to work, the establishment of support services and extended benefits is an essential component of the long-term effectiveness of the Work First New Jersey Program. Our experience tells us that these work supports are vital to the stability and sustainability of thousands of post-TANF recipients. We therefore recommend the inclusion of child-care and health care in the "standard of need" calculation. This would provide legislators and policy makers with a more accurate benchmark when considering the length of time necessary for transitional benefits to families working at low wages.

Secondly, in a 1999 report, *"The Real Cost of Living: The Self-Sufficiency Standard for New Jersey,"* Dr. Diana Pearce proposes a method for calculating the amount a family needs to meets its basic needs. Dr. Pearce "takes into account that many costs differ not only by family size and composition, but also by the age of the child." This standard also allows for regional and local variations in costs, which is of particular importance when calculating housing costs and to some extent child-care, health care and transportation. Dr. Pearce establishes separate standards for different family types in each of the 21 counties. Using this report (based on 1998 cost) a family of three (one adult, a schoolager, and a teenager) living in Camden County their monthly self-sufficiency income should be $1962. The proposed "standard of need" by the Department of Human Services for a family of three is $1465, $497 less than the self-sufficiency standard. A number of state programs administered by the DHS, including NJ Family Care and Supplemental Work Support program, identify 200–250 percent of the federal poverty level as the benchmark below which households are categorized as working poor, for a family of three this would translate to $2438 per month. In comparison then, the proposed standard of need understates the actual need for families and individuals living in New Jersey. We therefore recommend the usage of the method used by the self-sufficiency standard to calculate the real cost of living.

Finally, it is important to point out that there is a wide discrepancy between the current level of benefits and what is actually needed to live in some measure of human dignity. The New Jersey Catholic Conference believes that it is incumbent upon the Department of Human Services charged with establishing the standard of need to pursue vigorously a public assistance level to meet that standard.

The justice of a society is tested by its treatment of the poor. The Catholic Bishops urge the Commissioner to modify its proposed rules to include other items such as child-care, utilities and health care and to increase the proposed amount to reflect a more realistic level of need. We also urge the Commissioner upon the finalization of the "standard of need" rule to forcefully seek raising the cash benefit amount commensurate to the standard of need.

NOTES

1. Richard John Neuhaus, *The Naked Public Square: Religion and Democracy in America*, 2nd ed. (Grand Rapids, MI: Eerdmans, 1986), p. ix.

2. David Yamane, "Naked Public Square or Crumbling Wall of Separation? Evidence from Legislative Hearings in Wisconsin," *Review of Religious Research* 42 (2000): 175–92.

3. Jose Casanova, *Public Religions in the Modern World* (Chicago: University of Chicago Press, 1994), pp. 19, 37. The recent arguments in the Supreme Court's consideration of the phrase "under God" in the pledge of allegiance paradoxically helps to prove this point. According to the Bush administration's defense of the inclusion of "under God" in the pledge, the phrase is merely a ceremonial recognition of a past reality, not a positive affirmation of the current situation. As Casanova argues, the modern polity does not need such religious legitimation.

4. According to philosopher Paul Weithman, engagement with this question can be broken down into two broad categories. (1) Concerning political *outcomes*: can the government enforce religious codes of conduct? (2) Concerning political *inputs*: can people use religion as a basis for political decision-making? (See Weithman, *Religion and the Obligations of Citizenship* [Cambridge: Cambridge University Press, 2002], pp. 1–2.)

I consider the first category a *constitutional* issue and the second category a *philosophical-political* issue. The second category is my concern here. Although some consider the question of inputs a legal question concerning the separation of church and state (cf. Michael Perry, *Under God? Religious Faith and Liberal Democracy* [Cambridge: Cambridge University Press, 2003], pt. 1), it seems to me that the First Amendment protects fairly well the right of citizens to express religious views freely in public. The question is not whether these individuals have a *legal right* to express religious views but whether as good citizens they *ought* to exercise those rights.

5. Richard Rorty, "Religion as a Conversation-Stopper," *Common Knowledge* 3 (1994): 1–6.

6. Weithman, *Religion and the Obligations of Citizenship*, pp. 6, 11.

7. Christopher Eberle, *Religious Conviction in Liberal Politics* (Cambridge: Cambridge University Press, 2002), pp. 187, 196, 73.

8. Michael Perry's movement from an "exclusionist" to a more "inclusionist" position on the role of religion in politics can be seen in comparing his 1991 book, *Love and Power: The Role of Religion and Morality in American Politics* (New York: Oxford University Press), to his recent *Under God? Religious Faith and American Democracy* (Cambridge: Cambridge University Press, 2003).

9. Nicholas Wolterstorff, "The Role of Religion in Decision and Discussion of Political Issues," in *Religion in the Public Square: The Place of Religious Convictions in Political Debate* (Lanham, MD: Rowman & Littlefield, 1997); Eberle, *Religious Conviction in Liberal Politics*.

10 Perry, *Under God?*, p. 41. See also Stephen Carter, *The Culture of Disbelief: How American Law and Politics Trivialize Religious Devotion* (New York: Basic Books, 1993).

11. Jeffrey Stout, *Ethics After Babel: The Language of Morals and Their Discontents* (Boston: Beacon, 1988).

12. Christopher Beem, *The Necessity of Politics: Reclaiming American Public Life* (Chicago: University of Chicago Press, 1999).

13. Eberle, *Religious Conviction in Liberal Politics*, p. 188.

14. Weithman, *Religion and the Obligations of Citizenship*, p. 3.

15. Eberle, *Religious Conviction in Liberal Politics*, p. 10.

16. Robert Wuthnow, *The Restructuring of American Religion: Society and Faith Since World War II* (Princeton, NJ: Princeton University Press, 1988), p. 112.

17. Robert Wuthnow, *Producing the Sacred: An Essay on Public Religion* (Urbana, IL: University of Illinois Press, 1994), pp. 92, 155.

18. Hertzke, *Representing God in Washington: The Role of Religious Lobbies in the American Polity* (Knoxville, TN: University of Tennessee Press, 1988), p. 5.

19. It is certainly not the case that achieving political victories (passage or killing of legislation, inclusion or exclusion of amendments to bills, etc.) is always the goal of religious advocacy organizations. The United States Catholic Conference Office of Government Liaison, for example, distinguishes between "lobbying" and "witnessing" on different issues. Lobbying efforts are those in which "the USCC expects to commit all appropriate lobbying efforts to amend, pass or defeat specific legislation," while witnessing takes place on those issues on which "the USCC expects to take a formal position but does not intend to commit additional efforts to influence its disposition by Congress" (United States Catholic Conference, Office of Government Liaison, "Legislative Program: 105th Congress," February 1997).

20. Hertzke, *Representing God in Washington*, pp. 162, 196, 88.

21. Matthew Moen, "From Revolution to Evolution: The Changing Nature of the Christian Right," *Sociology of Religion* 55 (1994): 345–58, and Brian Steensland, "The Hydra and the Swords: Social Welfare and Mainline Advocacy, 1964–2000," pp. 213–36 in Robert Wuthnow and John Evans, eds., *The Quiet Hand of God: Faith-Based Activism and the Public Role of Mainline Protestantism* (Berkeley: University of California Press, 2002).

22. Kay Schlozman and John Tierney, *Organized Interests and American Democracy* (New York: Harper & Row, 1986), p. 150, table 7.1; Daniel Hofrenning, *In Washington But Not Of It: The Prophetic Politics of Religious Lobbyists* (Philadelphia: Temple University Press, 1995), p. 130, table 11; Anthony Nownes and Patricia Freeman, "Interest Group Activity in the States," *Journal of Politics* 60 (1998), table 2.

23. Although 100 percent of state Catholic conferences report offering testimony in public hearings before their state governments, only 62 percent made formal written copies of their testimony available to me for this study. Some conference directors indicated that they testify from notes or speak from memory, a couple were so new on the job that they had no testimony to provide, and others simply did not respond to my request for testimony.

Of those who did, five provided testimony on all four issues, eight on three of four, two on two of four, and six on one of four. The analysis in this chapter is based on 54 pieces of testimony from 21 conferences.

24. Although *cultural legitimation* is divided into two categories (*secular legitimations* and *civil religious legitimations*), in this chapter I do not fully consider this distinction. But see my article "Naked Public Square or Crumbling Wall of Separation?" See also Michele Dillon, "Cultural Differences in the Abortion Discourse of the Catholic Church: Evidence from Four Countries," *Sociology of Religion* 57 (1996): 25–36.

25. All told, 186 legitimations were coded from the 54 pieces of testimony analyzed. The number of legitimations in a given statement ranged from a low of one (seen in two cases) to a high of seven (also seen in two cases). The modal number of legitimations given was four (seen in 16 cases). Coding of the testimony was initially done independently by the author and a trained student assistant. A random sample of 10 pieces of testimony were coded and yielded a very high intercoder reliability score of .94 (Pearson's r), so the remaining 44 pieces of testimony were coded solely by the assistant. My thanks to Jennifer Smith for her intelligent and diligent work on this project.

26. Patrick L. Anderson, "A Hand Up for Michigan Workers: Creating a State Earned Income Tax Credit," prepared for the Michigan Catholic Conference by Anderson Economic Group, LLC, October 2002.

27. Transmittal letter for EITC report by Sr. Monica Kostielney, R.S.M., president and CEO, Michigan Catholic Conference.

28. Richard Rorty, "Religion in the Public Square: A Reconsideration," *Journal of Religious Ethics* 31 (2003): 143, 147. His reconsideration was prompted by Nicholas Wolterstorff, "Why We Should Reject What Liberalism Tells Us about Speaking and Acting for Religious Reasons," pp. 162–81 in Paul Weithman, ed., *Religion and Contemporary Liberalism* (Notre Dame: University of Notre Dame Press, 1997).

29. Richard Fenn, *Liturgies and Trials: The Secularization of Religious Language* (Oxford: Basil Blackwell, 1982), p. 118.

30. Steven D. Smith, "The 'Secular,' the 'Religious,' and the 'Moral': What Are We Talking About?" *Wake Forest Law Review* 36, no. 2 (2001), p. 508.

Conclusion

Catholic Political Advocacy in
Secular Society: Future Challenges

On January 16, 2003, the Vatican's Congregation for the Doctrine of the Faith made public a "Doctrinal Note on Some Questions Regarding the Participation of Catholics in Political Life."[1] The note was translated into six languages including English and addressed to the bishops of the Catholic Church, to Catholic politicians, and to all Catholic laity in democratic societies. Although the document defies simple summary, attention in the United States quickly focused on certain passages connecting lawmaking and church teaching:

> John Paul II, continuing the constant teaching of the Church, has reiterated many times that those who are directly involved in lawmaking bodies have a *"grave and clear obligation to oppose"* any law that attacks human life. For them, as for every Catholic, it is impossible to promote such laws or to vote for them. . . . In this context, it must be noted also that a well-formed Christian conscience does not permit one to vote for a political program or an individual law which contradicts the fundamental contents of faith and morals. (no. 4)

This same passage speaks of "fundamental and inalienable ethical demands" with respect to laws concerning abortion and euthanasia, embryonic experimentation, homosexuality and divorce, parents' right to educate their children, the protection of minors, "freedom from modern forms of slavery (drug abuse and prostitution, for example)," religious freedom, "the development of an economy that is at the service of the human person and of the common good," and peace. But the timing of the document's release, at least in the United States, made it inevitable that it would be interpreted primarily through the lens of abortion politics. The doctrinal note appeared one week before the thirtieth anniversary of the U.S. Supreme Court's decision legalizing abortion in *Roe v. Wade*.[2]

Significantly, the doctrinal note prescribed no punishments for those who violated the principles it advanced. Still, its release seemed to embolden some American bishops. For example, Bishop William Wiegand of Sacramento—in a Mass marking the thirtieth anniversary of *Roe v. Wade*—suggested that then–California governor Gray Davis and any Catholic supporting abortion rights should "choose of his own volition to abstain from receiving holy Communion until he has a change of heart." It was also reported in the media, though neither confirmed nor denied by the parties involved, that Bishop Robert Carlson of Sioux Falls wrote a letter to South Dakota senator Tom Daschle instructing him to stop calling himself a Catholic in good standing because of his support of abortion rights. The most dramatic moment, however, came the following January when Bishop Raymond Burke of La Crosse, Wisconsin, made public a notification that he signed in November 2003 concerning Catholic politicians from his diocese. In the notification, Burke declared, "A Catholic legislator who supports procured abortion or euthanasia, after knowing the teaching of the Church, commits a manifestly grave sin which is a cause of most serious scandal to others. . . . Therefore, in accord with the norm of can. 915 [of the Code of Canon Law], Catholic legislators, who are members of the faithful of the Diocese of La Crosse and who continue to support procured abortion or euthanasia may not present themselves to receive Holy Communion. They are not to be admitted to Holy Communion, should they present themselves, until such time as they publicly renounce their support of these most unjust practices." Other bishops followed Burke's lead in various ways, including New Orleans bishop Alfred Hughes, who wrote that "when Catholic officials openly support the taking of human life in abortion, euthanasia, or the destruction of human embryos, they are no longer faithful members in the Church and should not partake of holy Communion." Later in the spring, Archbishop John Myers of Newark and Bishop Michael Sheridan of Colorado Springs issued pastoral statements dealing with abortion and communion.[3] Debate over the wisdom and propriety of these bishops' actions simmered throughout 2004, fueled by the candidacy of Democratic Party nominee and abortion rights supporter John Kerry, who was seeking to become the first Roman Catholic since John F. Kennedy to be elected president of the United States. Upon his installation as archbishop of St. Louis in February 2004, the former bishop of La Crosse, Raymond Burke, made clear that candidate Kerry should not present himself for communion in his archdiocese.

As I discussed in chapter 1, the way the bishops of the United States have engaged public life has changed over time in response to social and political developments. It is possible that the individual engagement of Burke and others marks a new era in the dominant mode of engagement—a mode that would actually be a throwback to the localized engagement that characterized the early history of the church in America. But it is important to note an obvious fact that was lost in what Jon Stewart, host of Comedy Central's *Daily Show*, called "Wafer Madness": The vast majority of Catholic bishops in the United States—including prominent conservatives like Cardinals Justin Rigali of Philadelphia and Edward Egan of New York—remained silent on the issue. Others, like Cardinals William Keeler of Baltimore and Theodore McCarrick of Washington, said they would not use communion as a sanction against dissenting Catholic politicians. Indeed, those willing to make public pronouncements against dissenting Catholic politicians constituted well less than 10 percent of the 275 active bishops in the United States. For now at least, it appears to me that Archbishop Burke's engagement is the exception rather than the rule.

Without question, examining exceptional cases such as these can help us to understand what is ultimately at stake when religion and politics converge. At the same time, as a sociologist I am interested in more general patterns of engagement between religious faith and democratic politics. In this respect, despite all of the heat generated by the Great Communion Controversy of 2004, these incidents fail to shed much light on the broader role that the church plays in politics today. Like the buzz surrounding the legendary questioning of New York governor Mario Cuomo by Cardinal John O'Connor, the actions of a few bishops in 2004 generated so much attention precisely because they were so exceptional. The dominant, everyday reality of the bishops' involvement in politics is more mundane and therefore

garners less attention, especially at the state level. As I said at the out-
set, a major goal of this book is to divulge the secret that is the state
Catholic conferences. It does so by examining their history and organization, the issues they engage, their bases of legitimacy, and
how they bring their religious arguments into the public square.
These descriptive elements are framed by a broader theoretical concern with the question of secularization.

A NEO-SECULARIZATION PERSPECTIVE ON RELIGION AND POLITICS

Any attempt to address the relationship between religion and politics
must be undertaken with an eye to the broader issue of the place of
religion in society generally. This has been a central concern of sociologists from the classical period to the present. It has most often
been treated under the rubric of "secularization," which has been part
and parcel of the sociological lexicon since the discipline's inception.
But in recent years, several sociologists of religion have launched a
wholesale assault on the reality of secularization, prompting me to
criticize those who had prematurely declared the death of secularization theory. Shortly after my initial defense, Rodney Stark once again
wrote secularization theory's obituary, in the cleverly titled article
"Secularization, R.I.P."[4] So, once again, I find myself coming to the sociological cemetery to declare the decedent buried alive.

The "neo-secularization" perspective I favor is rooted in the earliest
understanding of the term "secularization," which was initially used
"to denote the removal of territory or property from the control of ecclesiastical authorities. In this sense, secularization means the disen-
gagement of religion from political life—the classic instance is the
separation of church and state—and the sundering of religion from
aesthetics so that art need no longer bend to moral norms but can follow its own impulses wherever they lead. In short, it is the shrinkage
of institutional authority over the spheres of public life, the retreat to
a private world where religions have authority only over their follow-
ers, and not over any other section of the polity or society."[5] This view
draws attention back to the foundational insight in sociology that I
discussed in the introduction: the idea that the development of modern society is characterized by institutional differentiation. In a highly

differentiated (and, hence, secular) society like the United States, the norms, values, and practices of the religious sphere have only an indirect influence on other spheres such as business, politics, leisure, and education. Put briefly, religion, under these secularized conditions, "can at best be politically relevant but no longer politically dominant."[6] Recall the story of the governor and the archbishop that opened this book.

But institutional differentiation is only half the equation, especially when we consider the religion-politics nexus. Secularization does not simply place constraints on religious activity in politics; it also enables some religious activity. This double-movement of secularization captures *both* the broad historical movement toward a decline in the scope of religious authority vis-à-vis secular authorities *and* the re-emergence of religious organizations in the political sphere under secularized conditions. Put more concretely, under conditions of societal-level secularization, where the scope of religious authority over institutions such as courts and legislatures has diminished, religious groups that seek to be effectively involved in these institutions are constrained to work in ways that articulate with and are accommodative of the reality of a secular society. My overall argument is that when state Catholic conferences represent the Catholic Church in state politics, they do so under secular conditions that constrain and enable their involvement.

As we saw in chapter 2, state Catholic conferences organizationally are best characterized as dual structures. This dual structure is already well adapted to the secular political system because under it the church's authority structure—bishops and priests—is not principally responsible for its political advocacy. Rather, the agency structure—the "secretariat" staffed overwhelmingly by lay professionals—carries out the church's direct advocacy work. Over the history of state Catholic conferences, the staff secretariats have become more professionalized and better adapted to the legislative environment by hiring personnel who are experienced in the law and state government. That this pays political dividends was demonstrated in chapter 4, which explored the multiple bases of legitimacy of state Catholic conferences in light of the priest sexual abuse scandal. In the end, state Catholic conferences are welcomed into the state legislative arena because they play by the secular rules of the political game, and they succeed to the extent that they play by those rules.

To say that state Catholic conferences adapt to the secular political environment is not to say that they have "sold out" to secularity. State Catholic conferences and their staff remain firmly grounded in the prophetic mission of the church, while taking a pragmatic approach to the public policy process. In chapters 3 and 5, we saw how the state Catholic conferences promote, in a partisan political system, a wildly diverse agenda that is held together by a concern for the dignity of the human person. Chapter 3 showed that conference staff are closely attuned to the political possibilities of the moment and use their nonpartisan "consistent life ethic" as a resource to build credibility and relationships with legislators. In this way, they build and conserve their precious political capital. The analysis of testimony in chapter 5 documented the frequent use of civil religious and secular arguments by state Catholic conference staff, either alone or in conjunction with specifically religious arguments. This reflects the recognition by the staff of the need to accommodate to the pluralistic, secular public square in which they operate. The words of Pope John Paul II himself provide the best summary of the way state Catholic conferences argue in the public square: "The Church proposes; she imposes nothing."[7] This is a reality of secular society that the Catholic Church has come to embrace over time.

FUTURE CHALLENGES

At least three potential problems loom on the horizon for state Catholic conferences, none of which are unique to the conferences. As we will see, they are broader issues being faced by the Catholic Church as a whole as it seeks to find its way in an increasingly secular world. Episcopal conferences face challenges from above, from below, and from without.

From Above

The ecclesiological justification for episcopal conferences can be found in the theology of collegiality, the idea that the bishops should act together to "express their communion" and "prolong the very life of the college of the apostles."[8] Under the pontificate of John Paul II, however, some in the church have increasingly questioned whether

episcopal conferences constitute a legitimate form of episcopal collegiality. Joseph Cardinal Ratzinger, head of the Vatican's Congregation for the Doctrine of the Faith, has a particularly dim view of the
conferences in this regard. Ratzinger writes, "We must not forget that
the episcopal conferences have no theological basis, they do not be-
long to the indispensable structure of the Church as willed by Christ,"
and therefore, "no episcopal conference, as such, has a teaching mission; its documents have no weight of their own save that of the consent given to them by the individual bishops."[9] This concern about
episcopal conferences led the 1985 Extraordinary Assembly of the
Synod of Bishops to call "for a fuller and more profound study of the
theological and, consequently, the juridical status of episcopal conferences, and above all of the issue of their doctrinal authority." The
result of the Vatican's study of the issue was an Apostolic Letter—
Apostolos Suos ("On the Theological and Juridical Nature of Episcopal Conferences")—issued by John Paul in 1998.[10]

The fact that the letter was not issued until 13 years after the Synod
suggests much controversy surrounding the study and its conclu-
sions.[11] Nevertheless, the major conclusion of the letter was that, "at
the level of particular Churches grouped together by geographic areas (by countries, regions, etc.), the bishops in charge do not exercise
pastoral care jointly with collegial acts equal to those of the college of
bishops." Thus, although national episcopal conferences are "a concrete application of collegial spirit (*affectus collegialis*) . . . this terri-
torially based exercise of the episcopal ministry never takes on the
collegial nature proper to the actions of the order of bishops as such,
which alone holds supreme power over the whole Church."[12] In
short, episcopal authority resides with the all of the bishops worldwide collectively, in communion with the bishop of Rome. That authority is then delegated to individual bishops in their own dioceses.
According to Vatican II's "Dogmatic Constitution on the Church" (*Lumen Gentium*), individual bishops "are the visible principle and foundation of unity in their particular churches. . . . For this reason the individual bishops represent each his own church. . . . The individual
bishops, who are placed in charge of particular churches, exercise
their pastoral government over the portion of the People of God committed to their care" (no. 23).[13]

Concern that episcopal conferences usurp authority properly exer-
cised by the college of bishops or individual bishops (in communion

with the Pope) has been present since the founding of the National Catholic Welfare Conference. As noted in chapter 1, several bishops, led by Cardinal William Henry O'Connell of Boston, actively opposed a national episcopal organization for the United States in the 1920s. That Bishop Raymond Burke did not coordinate his actions against dissenting Catholic politicians with either the Wisconsin Catholic Conference or the United States Conference of Catholic Bishops reflects the continuing sentiment among some that episcopal conferences are not a legitimate vehicle to express the teaching authority of the church—a sentiment affirmed by *Apostolos Suos*.

Thus far, this challenge to episcopal conferences has not trickled down to the state level. If it does, state Catholic conferences will have less to fall back on than the national conference. The Second Vatican Council's "Decree on Bishops" (*Christus Dominus*) and the related canons of the 1983 Code of Canon Law speak explicitly only about national and regional episcopal conferences. Although analogous to national conferences in many ways, state-level episcopal conferences are *non-canonical* entities. In his doctoral dissertation, *The State Catholic Conference: A New Development in Interecclesial Cooperation in the United States*, Michael Sheehan notes that "membership in the State Conference is voluntary for each diocese, but there is a certain moral pressure on each bishop to cooperate with one another for the good of the Church."[14] This moral pressure continues. At this point, I know of no instance in which a bishop has ceased participating in an already existing conference. In the short run, at least, common practical, political, and pastoral concerns should continue to hold the conferences together. But those interested in the future role of the Catholic Church in American political life do well to keep an eye on this dual dynamic of centralization (in Rome) and decentralization (in individual dioceses) that threaten to diminish the role of intermediate organizations like national and intra-national episcopal conferences.

From Below

The second challenge to the ability of state Catholic conferences to represent the church comes from the diversity of positions held by lay Catholics on public policy issues. Legislators are acutely aware of the (at times large) gap between the positions being advocated by the bishops and the opinions of the laity. Even as the bishops articulate countercultural positions on life issues and economic justice, Catholics increasingly blend into the American public attitudinally. Although the gap is not as large for those Catholics who are most committed to the institutional church (e.g., those who attend Mass most regularly), the proportion of Catholics who are so committed is shrinking. Consequently, the bishops often appear to public officials as "generals without troops."[15]

Recognizing the importance of grassroots support, state Catholic conferences do try to mobilize the laity in support of their legislative initiatives. The two most common vehicles for this are "lobby days" and advocacy networks. Three-quarters of state Catholic conferences sponsor lobby days—programs designed to bring lay Catholics to the state capitol for education and advocacy. The Wisconsin Catholic Conference's website describes their lobby day, Catholics at the Capitol, this way: "Convened in the spring of each new legislative session (odd numbered years), Catholics at the Capitol helps you understand the legislative process and enhances your advocacy skills. Through workshops and networking, Catholics from across the state join together to bring a united Catholic voice to the Capitol." Similarly, the Maryland Catholic Conference held its twenty-first annual lobby night in 2005. Catholics from around the state converge on Annapolis each President's Day for briefings and breakout sessions on pressing issues followed by visits to their legislators.

Many conferences also have advocacy networks in place to mobilize grassroots support for legislative initiatives. To some extent, these networks allow conferences to work around the broader issue posed by a divided laity. For example, Desmond Ryan set up the Indiana Catholic Action Network (I-CAN) shortly after he was named executive director of the Indiana Catholic Conference in 1978. The bishop of each of Indiana's five dioceses appoints a coordinator to build and organize the network for his diocese. The Indiana Catholic Conference sends newsletters to I-CAN members that outline the church's position on issues and indicates the status of legislative activity on them. When key votes are scheduled to take place in the state legislature, an "action alert" is disseminated by the conference staff through network telephone trees. In 2003, there were about 5,000 I-CAN members, of course with diverse interests. As Ryan observed, "it's hard to have one organization getting people involved on all issues. Most people have a special issue of interest, and that's always been a concern of mine.

I built the network with the idea that we would alert *everybody* to *everything* and then individuals would make a choice about what they would act on." During my visit to the Maryland Catholic Conference, Executive Director Dick Dowling spoke at length about how he is dealing with this same situation. "My dream is of a Catholic faithful that is a seamless garment constituency. They would understand and feel passionately about all the issues. But the fact is that they don't. The network I *wanted* to build was a single network, one body that could be trusted to be aggressive on the whole panoply of church issues. But it's not. . . . Reluctantly, over the years, I've realized that." So, rather than having everyone in a single grassroots network wading through material until they find something on the issues they care about, the Maryland Catholic Conference is increasingly organizing single-issue constituencies. Dowling continues, "If you want to get the best results, you have to organize a constituency about something it wants, and so more and more we've done that. Mary Ellen Russell has organized the Maryland Federation of Catholic School Families. Nancy Fortier is doing a wonderful job organizing her anti-abortion constituency. It's the same with the death penalty and social justice matters. I wish we didn't have to, but we do."

Although state Catholic conferences can continue to mobilize segments of the Catholic population which are supportive of the church's positions on specific issues, it is hard-pressed to mobilize "the Catholic community" politically, because no such community exists. Even worse for the conferences, lay Catholics as individuals and as organized movements feel freer than ever to openly dissent from the bishops in the public square. Catholics for a Free Choice comes immediately to mind on this score. The divisions in the Catholic community and the increasingly open dissent raise the question of who the state Catholic conferences actually represent. Many conferences are careful to claim that they represent "the Catholic Bishops" (Connecticut) or "the Catholic bishops and the Catholic dioceses" (Pennsylvania) in the state. Some portray themselves more broadly as "the official voice of the Catholic Church" (Michigan, Kansas) or "the official voice of the Catholic community" (California) in the state. In the latter cases, the modifier "official" already points to the possibility that there may be other Catholic voices in the public square. Some conferences forgo the qualifier and simply claim to be "the public policy agency of the Catholic Church" (Missouri) or "the public policy voice of the Catholic Church" (Minnesota) in the state.[16] With or without the qualification, these claims to represent "the church" will increasingly ring hollow if the Catholic laity does not stand with the bishops on issues across the consistent ethic of life.

That said, an even more fundamental problem than people dissenting from the bishops is people ignoring them. The findings of a survey conducted by sociologists James Davidson and Dean Hoge in the wake of the sexual abuse scandal suggest reason for concern here. The fall 2003 survey of a nationally representative sample of Catholics reveals that most Catholics do not know and do not care about either their individual bishop or the bishops collectively. Well less than a majority of Catholics (41 percent) in the survey were able to provide a name when asked if they could name their local bishop (and surely the percentage that *correctly* named their bishop was lower). Concerning the bishops collectively, Davidson and Hoge report, "When asked how much they know about U.S. bishops and their activities, only 7 percent of the sample said 'a great deal' and 24 percent said 'some.' Forty-three percent said they did not know very much, and 25 percent said they know 'nothing' about the bishops." From this, Davidson and Hoge conclude, "the bishops are not an important reference point in the faith life of most Catholics."[17] Of course, this is not just a political problem for the bishops; it is a challenge that goes to the very heart of the Catholic Church and what it means to be Catholic today. But the political implications are evident nonetheless.

From Without

One of the biggest challenges facing state Catholic conferences comes from outside the church and concerns the question of institutional integrity. There is a concerted effort underway, especially at the state level, to implement public policies that threaten the constitutional right of Catholic institutions to function in accord with church teaching. These policies create pressures on religious institutions, according to USCCB general counsel Mark Chopko, "to choose between religious identity and serving our communities." In a speech at Catholic University in 2003, Chopko outlined four such pressures.[18] In the interest of space, I will focus only on one: pressure to require all employers—including Catholic institutions—to provide contraceptive coverage in their health care or prescription drug plans.

This pressure comes most directly from a systematic effort led by the Planned Parenthood Federation of America to pass "contraceptive equity" legislation—also known as "pill bills."[19] Planned Parenthood and its allies maintain that an employer's policy of excluding coverage for prescription contraception from a comprehensive employee health plan discriminates against women because only women use prescription contraceptives. In 1997, Planned Parenthood helped draft and promote the federal Equity in Prescription Insurance and Contraceptive Coverage Act. Although this bill has yet to pass in Congress, its advocates have had more success in the states. In 1998, Maryland became the first state to pass "contraceptive equity" legislation.[20] Since then, 20 other states have followed suit, and in August 2004 Wisconsin's attorney general opined that the states Fair Employment Act already requires equitable access to contraceptive coverage for women. Furthermore, at the end of 2004, 12 more states had contraceptive equity bills pending.[21]

According to the Alan Guttmacher Institute, of the 21 states that have passed pill bills, 12 exempt religious employers and one (Missouri) allows religious and secular employers to claim an exemption based on moral, ethical, or religious grounds.[22] In fact, the religious "exemption" in these laws can be drawn so narrowly that they exclude from their definition Catholic institutions that provide health care, education, and social services. Under the laws passed in California and New York State, for example, the exemption for religious employers "is limited to those institutions which teach their own, and serve their own, and hire their own adherents." But as Mark Chopko points out, "Under this definition, Mother Teresa's Missionaries of Charity are 'secular' employers because they don't limit their care of AIDS victims to Catholics."[23] In fact, Catholic Charities organizations would be required to choose either to provide no prescription drug coverage to its employees or to include contraceptive coverage in their plans. Catholic Charities of Sacramento challenged California's Women's Contraceptive Equity Act in the state court, claiming it violated the constitutionally protected right to free exercise of religion by requiring a religious institution to pay for something that it deems immoral. In March 2004, the California Supreme Court ruled 6–1 against Catholic Charities, and that October the U.S. Supreme Court declined to take the case, without comment.[24]

This threat to the integrity of Catholic institutions goes beyond just "pill bills." Planned Parenthood and its allies promote contraception as "a basic health need for women."[25] From the perspective of state Catholic conferences, this is where the slippery slope comes in, because from Planned Parenthood's perspective, so is abortion. Many in the church will be appalled but not shocked when the day comes that a Catholic university is required by law to provide insurance that pays for abortion services and a Catholic hospital is required by law to provide those services, in the name of gender equity in basic health care.

How are state Catholic conferences to face these challenges from without? To be sure, they are facing an uphill political battle. The Catholic Church is required by law and its own self-understanding to stay out of electoral politics. But its opponents in this case, most especially Planned Parenthood, are not similarly restrained. In fact, in addition to the Planned Parenthood Action Fund and the Planned Parenthood Federal PAC, Planned Parenthood Votes is one of the largest Section 527 "stealth PACs" in the country. How is the Catholic Church going to protect its institutional integrity under these unequal political conditions? For now I think more church leaders are feeling the pull of involvement in electoral politics. When it comes to maintaining the fundamental identity of Catholic institutions, many will feel that the church cannot afford to be nonpartisan. Without helping to elect legislators who will respect the free exercise of religion, the church will remain at a great disadvantage in this fight. So, just as Planned Parenthood looks to Democrats as allies in this fight, it is natural for the Catholic Church to look to Republicans. This mirrors on the organizational level the same push away from the Democratic Party and pull toward the Republican Party that many Catholics feel as individuals. Ideally, Catholics are a "pilgrim people"—politically homeless in America's bi-partisan system.[26] But the realities of American political life create strong pressures for Catholics and the Catholic Church to find a home in one or the other existing party. For most of the history of Catholics in America, that home was in the Democratic Party. In the foreseeable future, it may be the Republican Party. As Denver archbishop Charles Chaput told the *New York Times*, "We are not with the Republican Party. They are with us." The fact that 52 percent of Catholics who voted in the 2004 presidential election cast their ballots for the evangelical Republican George W. Bush, compared to 47 percent for the Catholic Democrat John Kerry, is significant in this regard. Of course, state Catholic conferences cannot officially ally themselves with either party. In their most recent election year statement, *Faithful Citizenship: A Catholic Call to Political Responsibility*, the U.S. bishops reaffirmed that "the Church cannot be a chaplain for any one party or cheerleader for any candidate."[27] But with pressures mounting, they may informally become more closely connected to Republicans.

CONCLUSION

It is beyond my competence as an analyst to speculate how well state Catholic conferences will face these challenges in the future. It is difficult enough simply to convey accurately and adequately the current reality of these organizations. But the history of episcopal conferences in general and state Catholic conferences in particular is one of evolution and adaptation to the cultural and political environment within which they work. I do not doubt that they will continue to evolve and adapt as necessary to realize the goal of faithfully and effectively representing the Catholic Church's material and ideal interests before the state governments. In the end, as a Catholic myself, I can only hope the state Catholic conferences—and the church as a whole—continue to attempt the same balancing act that the U.S. bishops described in their 1995 statement on political responsibility: "The challenge for our Church is to be principled without being ideological, to be political without being partisan, to be civil without being soft, to be involved without being used. Our moral framework does not easily fit the categories of left or right, Republican or Democrat. We are called to measure every party and movement by how its agenda touches human life and dignity."

NOTES

1. The note was approved by Pope John Paul II on November 21, 2002, and dated November 24, 2002—the feast of Christ the King, instituted by Pope Pius XI in 1925 to counter totalitarian political movements in Europe. See Raymond De Souza, "Vatican to Catholic Politicians: Vote Pro-Life," *National Catholic Register*, 26 January–1 February 2003.

2. Daniel Williams, "Pope Admonishes Catholic Politicians," *Washington Post*, 17 January 2003.

3. Wayne Laugesen, "Calif. Bishop to Gov. Davis: Pick Abortion or Communion," *National Catholic Register*, 2–8 February 2003; Tim Drake, "What Did Bishop Carlson Write to Sen. Daschle?" *National Catholic Register*, 4–10

May 2003; "Two Archbishops Challenge Lawmakers on Abortion," *America*, 2 February 2004; David Kocieniewski, "Governor Puts Communion Aside after Upsetting New Jersey Bishops," *New York Times*, 6 May 2004; Mindy Sink, "At Mass, Politics Squeezes into the Pews," *New York Times*, 17 May 2004.

4. David Yamane, "Secularization on Trial: In Defense of a Neo-Secularization Paradigm," *Journal for the Scientific Study of Religion* 36 (March 1997): 107–120. At the time, R. Stephen Warner was particularly exuberant about the death of secularization theory in his otherwise magnificent essay "Work in Progress Toward a New Paradigm for the Sociological Study of Religion in the United States," *American Journal of Sociology* 98 (1993): 1044–93. For Rodney Stark's later criticism, see "Secularization, R.I.P.," *Sociology of Religion* 60, no. 3 (1999): 249–74.

5. Daniel Bell, "The Return of the Sacred? The Argument on the Future of Religion," pp. 324–54 in *The Winding Passage: Essays and Sociological Journeys, 1960–1980* (Basic Books: New York, 1980), pp. 331–32.

6. Wolfgang Schluchter, *Rationalism, Religion, and Domination: A Weberian Perspective* (Berkeley: University of California Press, 1989), p. 263.

7. John Paul II, *Redemptoris Missio* ("On the Permanent Validity of the Church's Missionary Mandate"), 7 December 1990, no. 39.

8. John Paul II, *Apostolos Suos* ("On the Theological and Juridical Nature of Episcopal Conferences"), 21 May 1998, no. 3.

9. Joseph Cardinal Ratzinger, *The Ratzinger Report: An Exclusive Interview of the State of the Church* (San Francisco: Ignatius Press, 1985), pp. 59–60.

10. *Apostolos Suos*, no. 7.

11. Indeed, a book of essays engaging a 1988 Vatican working paper on the issue was already published in 1989, nearly a decade before the final letter was released. See Thomas Reese, S.J., ed., *Episcopal Conferences: Historical, Canonical, and Theological Studies* (Washington, DC: Georgetown University Press, 1989).

12. *Apostolos Suos*, nos. 10, 12.

13. See also *Catechism of the Catholic Church* (Washington, DC: United States Catholic Conference–Libreria Editrice Vaticana, 1997), no. 886.

14. Rev. Michael J. Sheehan, *The State Catholic Conference: A New Development in Interecclesial Cooperation in the United States*, (an excerpt from a dissertation presented for the degree of Doctor of Canon Law, Pontifical Lateran University, Rome, 1971), p. 58. See ch. 2, n. 1 for the location of this document.

15. The history of the National Catholic Welfare Conference reveals a failure to involve the laity from the start. Catholic historian Elizabeth McKeown has argued that "the Catholic laity remained a missing or mismanaged ingredient in the development of the NCWC." NCWC founder John Burke, C.S.P., warned the bishops not to neglect the important role the laity could play in

the battles of the day, but clericalist fears of lay empowerment won the day. Even the Knights of Columbus—not a dissenting organization, to put it mildly—refused to affiliate its membership with the NCWC. See Elizabeth McKeown, "The 'National Idea' in the History of the American Episcopal Conference," pp. 59–84 in Thomas Reese, ed., *Episcopal Conferences: Historical, Canonical, and Theological Studies* (Washington, DC: Georgetown University Press, 1989), p. 78.

16. "The Connecticut Catholic Conference is the public policy and advocacy office of the Catholic Bishops in Connecticut," http://www.ctcatholic.org; "The Pennsylvania Catholic Conference is the public affairs arm of Pennsylvania's Catholic bishops and the Catholic dioceses of Pennsylvania," http://www.pacatholic.org/about%20pcc/index.htm; "The Michigan Catholic Conference serves as the official voice of the Catholic Church in Michigan on matters of public policy," http://www.micatholicconference.org/general_info/; "The Kansas Catholic Conference serves as the official voice of the Catholic Church in Kansas on matters of public policy," http://www.kscathconf.org; "California Catholic Conference: Official Voice of the Catholic Community in California's Public Policy Arena," http://www.ca-catholic.org/; "The Missouri Catholic Conference is the public policy agency of the Catholic Church in our state," http://www.mocatholic.org/showpage.asp?PID=aboutus.htm; "The public policy voice of the Catholic Church in Minnesota," http://www.mncc.org/About%20MCC.htm. All websites accessed 9 December 2004.

17. James Davidson and Dean Hoge, "Catholics After the Scandal: A New Study's Major Findings," *Commonweal*, 19 November 2004, pp. 15–16. This is a significant problem for the bishops, but it would be wrong to conclude that the sexual abuse scandal *created* it. I rather agree with Peter Steinfels's assessment that the scandal simply brought the problem to the fore and exacerbated it. See his book *A People Adrift: The Crisis of the Roman Catholic Church in America* (New York: Simon & Schuster, 2003).

18. Mark Chopko, "Shaping the Church: Overcoming the Twin Challenges of Secularization and Scandal," *Catholic University Law Review* 53 (2003): 125–159.

19. See Planned Parenthood's "Fair Access to Contraception" project's website, http://www.covermypills.org. The other major organizations involved in this movement include the Coalition of Labor Union Women's "Contraceptive Equity Project," http://www.cluw.org/contraceptive.html; the Center for Reproductive Rights (formerly the Center for Reproductive Law and Policy), http://www.crlp.org/pri_contraception.html; and NARAL Pro-Choice America's Proactive Policy Institute. See NARAL's "The Contraception Report: A State-by-State Review of Access to Contraception" (Washington, DC: NARAL Foundation, 2001), available online at http://www.naral.org/ppi/pubs/contraception.cfm.

20. Also in 1998, contraceptive coverage for federal employees was included in the Treasury-Postal Appropriations Bill and signed into law by President Bill Clinton. Although President George W. Bush attempted to remove this coverage from later appropriations bills, it was restored by Congress and continues to be provided. See Planned Parenthood's online history, http://www.plannedparenthood.org/timeline/index.html (accessed 7 December 2004).

21. Planned Parenthood's "Fair Access to Contraception" project, http://www.covermypills.org/facts/ (accessed 9 December 2004). Proponents of "contraceptive equity" have also pursued the issue in the courts, claiming that failure to provide contraceptive coverage to women is a violation of Title VII of the 1964 Civil Rights Act. In June 2001, they received a favorable ruling from the United States District Court for the Western District of Washington at Seattle in the case of *Erickson v. Bartell Drug Co.* (2001 WL 649651 W.D.Wash. June 12, 2001).

22. Alan Guttmacher Institute, "Insurance Coverage of Contraceptives," http://www.guttmacher.org/statecenter/spibs/spib_ICC.pdf (accessed 8 December 2004).

23. Chopko, "Shaping the Church," p. 143.

24. Stephanie Strom, "Catholic Group is Told to Pay for Birth Control," *New York Times*, 2 March 2004; Bob Egelko, "High Court Declines Religious Dispute Over Contraceptives," *San Francisco Chronicle*, 5 October 2004.

25. Planned Parenthood's "Fair Access to Contraception Project," http://www.covermypills.org (accessed 8 December 2004).

26. Clarke Cochran, "The Pilgrim Community's Independent Voice," *America*, 3 December 2001, pp. 12–15.

27. Chaput interview with *New York Times*, 12 October 2004; Administrative Committee of the United States Conference of Catholic Bishops, *Faithful Citizenship: A Catholic Call to Political Responsibility* (Washington, DC: United States Conference of Catholic Bishops, 2003), p. 29.

Appendix

Supplemental Tables

Table A.1.   State Catholic Conferences and Their Dates of Establishment

Alaska Catholic Conference	1973
Arizona Catholic Conference	1973
California Catholic Conference	1972
Colorado Catholic Conference	1968
Connecticut Catholic Conference	1968
District of Columbia Catholic Conference	1995
Florida Catholic Conference	1969
Georgia Catholic Conference	1972
Hawaii Catholic Conference	1993
Illinois Catholic Conference[a]	1969
Indiana Catholic Conference	1966
Iowa Catholic Conference	1967
Kansas Catholic Conference	1967
Catholic Conference of Kentucky	1967
Louisiana Catholic Conference	1972
Maryland Catholic Conference	1967
Massachusetts Catholic Conference	1969
Michigan Catholic Conference[b]	1963
Minnesota Catholic Conference	1967
Missouri Catholic Conference	1967
Montana Catholic Conference	1969
Nebraska Catholic Conference	1969
Nevada Catholic Conference	2000
New Jersey Catholic Conference[c]	1969
New Mexico Catholic Conference	1991
New York State Catholic Conference[d]	1916
North Dakota Catholic Conference	1970
Catholic Conference of Ohio	1945
Oregon Catholic Conference	1978
Pennsylvania Catholic Conference	1960
Texas Catholic Conference	1963
Virginia Catholic Conference[e]	2004
Washington State Catholic Conference	1965
West Virginia Catholic Conference	1968
Wisconsin Catholic Conference	1968

Notes:
[a] According to Sheehan, was preceded by the Illinois Catholic Committee for Legislation "by at least twenty-five years."
[b] Was preceded by Catholic Charities in Michigan, begun in 1958.
[c] According to Sheehan, was "preceded by a lobby group begun in 1947."
[d] Formerly called the New York State Catholic Committee.
[e] Was founded too late to be included in this study.

Source: Michael Sheehan, "State Catholic Conferences," *The Jurist* 35 (1975), table 1, and my own State Catholic Conference Survey, 2002.

Table A.2.   Catholic Characteristics of States with No Catholic Conference in 2002

State	# of Dioceses (2002)	Catholic Population (1970)	% Catholic in State (1970)	Catholic Population (2001)	% Catholic in State (2001)
Alabama	2	82,346	2.4	156,915	3.5
Arkansas	1	55,293	2.8	93,480	3.6
Delaware (*)	1	126,125	14.3	205,000	18.0
Idaho (*)	1	52,182	7.0	130,500	9.9
Maine (*)	1	267,886	27.4	212,253	17.2
Mississippi	2	82,383	3.5	115,916	4.2
New Hampshire (*)	1	268,685	38.5	325,674	31.8
North Carolina (*)	2	64,243	1.1	296,922	3.8
Oklahoma	2	114,627	4.5	160,898	4.3
Rhode Island (*)	1	587,685	65.8	623,752	63.1
South Carolina	1	44,751	1.7	130,255	3.2
South Dakota (*)	2	138,700	21.0	156,727	21.5
Tennessee	3	90,595	2.3	186,823	3.4
Utah (*)	1	50,483	4.7	107,000	5.0
Vermont	1	141,193	32.8	148,712	25.1
Virginia	2	241,697	4.6	553,709	8.0
Wyoming	1	45,000	14.3	48,781	10.1
Average	1.47	144,345	14.6	214,901	13.9
Average for States with SCCs	4.38	1,254,767	23.0	1,662,591	21.6

Notes: Data are as of January 1, 2001, and are from The Official Catholic Directory, 2001. In states marked with an asterisk (*), a diocese is an affiliate member of the National Association of State Catholic Conference Directors.

Table A.3. State Catholic Conference Boards of Directors

State	1975	2003
Alaska	7 members: 3 ordinaries, 2 laymen, 1 laywoman, 1 sister	4 members: the bishops of Alaska
Arizona	9 members: 3 ordinaries, 1 cleric, 1 layperson from each diocese	18 members including the 3 bishops of the state
California	18 members: the bishops of California	Same. Currently 26 members.
Colorado	No formal board: the 3 bishops, their advisors, and the conference director set the policy.	The 4 bishops of Colorado are the board of governors. An administrative board advises on public policy issues.
Connecticut	17 members: 3 ordinaries, 2 auxiliaries, 4 from each of 3 dioceses	All diocesan bishops of the Latin church and the eparch of the Ukrainian church in the state of Connecticut
District of Columbia	N/A	The archbishop and auxiliary bishops of Washington
Florida	6 members: the bishops of Florida (called the board of trustees)	Same. Currently 10 members.
Georgia	Bylaws under revision at this time—the two bishops of Georgia provide policy direction at present.	The 2 bishops of Georgia provide policy direction at present.
Hawaii	N/A	9 members: 1 bishop, 1 deacon, 1 sister, 1 priest, 5 laypersons
Illinois	33 members: 11 bishops, 6 priests, laymen and laywomen (1 each from each diocese), 1 religious priest, 1 brother, 2 sisters	42 members: the bishops in the state of Illinois (20) plus a priest and 2 laypersons from each of the 6 dioceses. In addition, there are 4 Religious-at-Large members appointed. Only the 6 ordinaries are voting members.
Indiana	11 members: 6 bishops, 1 layperson from each diocese. Advisory council of 14 formulates policy recommendations for the board.	10 members: 5 bishops, 1 layperson from each diocese (diocesan coordinators)
Iowa	5 members: bishops of Iowa	27 members: voting members are the bishops of Iowa, active and retired (currently 6); non-voting members include: 1 priest, 1 layman, 1 laywoman, and 1 at-large member from each diocese; plus 4 women religious and 1 deacon
Kansas	8 members: 4 bishops, an elected diocesan education person, an elected diocesan social concerns person, an attorney, the executive director of the conference (called board of governors)	4 bishops and the executive director of the conference (called board of governors)

State		
Kentucky	Bishops of the state—conference at present under reorganization	4 members: the bishops of Kentucky
Louisiana	6 members: bishops of Louisiana	9 members: 7 ordinaries and 2 auxiliary bishops of Louisiana
Maryland	3 bishops of Maryland (including the archbishop of Washington and the bishop of Wilmington whose dioceses contain parts of Maryland)	Maryland-serving bishops and auxiliary bishops (including the Archdiocese of Washington, D.C., and the Diocese of Wilmington, Delaware, which contain parts of Maryland)
Massachusetts	Bishops of Massachusetts. Called the board of governors, the highest decision-making body. There is also a board of directors composed of the bishops and 4 other persons each selected by an ordinary.	The board of governors includes all residential bishops of the Latin church in Massachusetts. There is also a board of directors composed of the bishops and 4 other persons each selected by an ordinary
Michigan	14 members: 7 ordinaries, 5 laypersons, 1 priest, and 1 sister	Same
Minnesota	The bishops of Minnesota	Same
Missouri	The bishops of Missouri	Same
Montana	9 members: 2 bishops, 1 priest, 6 laypersons	11 voting members: 2 ordinaries, plus 2 laypersons, 1 religious sister, and 1 priest from each diocese, and 1 representative of the Knights of Columbus. Also, 3 non-voting (ex officio) members: Catholic Campaign for Human Development Director, Diocese of Great Falls-Billings Office of Social Justice & Peace Director, and Chancellor of the Diocese of Helena.
Nebraska	21 members: 3 ordinaries; 1 representative from each diocese in education, public affairs, pastoral life, social development; and 2 laypersons from each diocese	24 members: 3 ordinaries, 1 representative from each diocese in education, health, public affairs, pastoral life, social development, and 2 laypersons from each diocese
Nevada	N/A	The 2 bishops of Nevada
New Jersey	The bishops of New Jersey. The conference consists of the bishops and a strong advisory board that meets with the bishops.	The bishops of New Jersey, including the Byzantine and Syriac Catholic dioceses. There is also a Public Policy Committee that is composed of 36 clerical, lay, and religious members serving as an advisory board to the bishops.
New Mexico	N/A	3 members: The bishops of New Mexico

(continued)

Table A.3. (*continued*)

State	1975	2003
New York	The bishops of New York (called administrative board of the New York State Catholic Conference). The State Catholic Committee, a representative group, has a strong advisory role in the conference.	Same
North Dakota	5 members: 2 bishops, 3 laypersons	13 members: Acting bishops of the state (2), vicar general for each diocese (2), moderator of the curia or chancellor from each diocese (2), 3 persons from each diocese (6), and 1 member at large serving for a single term appointed alternatively from each diocese (1).
Ohio	The bishops of Ohio. Delegates of the diocesan priest senates are present for board meetings.	Every Roman Catholic Bishop exercising jurisdiction in Ohio, as well as the Bishops of the Parma Byzantine Eparchy, Romanian Catholic Diocese of Canton, and Ukranian Catholic Diocese of Parma. Delegates of the diocesan priest senates are present for board meetings.
Oregon	N/A	The archbishop of Portland in Oregon, the bishop of Baker, and any active bishops of these dioceses. A Roman Catholic priest chosen by consent of the archbishop of Portland and the bishop of Baker shall serve a (renewable) 3-year term. Retired bishops shall be honorary (non-voting) members. The board of directors meets jointly with a Public Policy Advisory Committee.
Pennsylvania	10 members: 8 Latin ordinaries, 2 Eastern Rite ordinaries (called board of governors). An administrative board composed of representatives from the dioceses has strong advisory capacity.	The board of governors comprises the local ordinary bishops of Pennsylvania dioceses, including the Philadelphia Ukrainian Catholic Archeparchy and Pittsburgh Byzantine Catholic Archdiocese.

Texas	Regular members: 11 ordinaries. Consultative members are the retired and auxiliary bishops, elected representatives of priest councils, sisters' councils, major superiors, lay delegates at large, and chairpersons of the 5 divisions through which the conference functions.	Ordinaries of Texas dioceses are the regular members and other bishops who serve or have served the church in Texas (and are still resident) are consultative members. Only regular members have a decisive vote on matters coming before the board of directors.
Washington	The bishops of Washington	The bishops of Washington (currently 4) and 3 representatives from each of the 3 dioceses, including at least 1 male and 1 female layperson from each diocese
West Virginia	N/A	The bishop of Wheeling-Charleston, the vicar general (who serves as conference director), and 2 lobbyists. The conference also has an advisory board made up of professional lay people in a variety of fields (e.g. school, business, legal, social).
Wisconsin	The highest decision-making body is the policy board. Members include the 8 bishops of the state (who form the board of directors), the executive board (5 members elected biannually by and from the general membership of the conference and the chairperson of the 3 commissions of the conference).	All bishops or administrators of the dioceses in Wisconsin, including auxiliary and retired bishops, constitute the board of directors

Source: For 1975, Michael Sheehan, "State Catholic Conferences," *The Jurist* 35 (1975): 451–53, table 4. For 2003, a survey of state Catholic conferences by the author and information available on the conferences' websites (see the listing provided by the National Association of State Catholic Conference Directors at http://www.nasccd.org/).

Table A.4. Change in State Laws Regarding Clergy as Mandatory Reporters of Child (Sexual) Abuse

Mandatory Reporters of Child Sexual Abuse?	Through 2001	Change in 2002–03	Change Failed in 2002–03
Clergy are mandatory reporters, with exemption for privileged communications (in the reporting law itself or in the state's rules of evidence or civil procedure).	ARIZONA, CALIFORNIA, CONNECTICUT, MAINE, MINNESOTA, MONTANA, NEVADA, NORTH DAKOTA, OREGON, PENNSYLVANIA	ALABAMA, ARKANSAS, COLORADO, ILLINOIS, LOUISIANA, MAINE, MASSACHUSETTS, MICHIGAN, MISSOURI, NEW MEXICO	ALASKA, HAWAII, IOWA (VETOED), NEW YORK, OHIO, SOUTH DAKOTA, VIRGINIA, WASHINGTON, WISCONSIN, SOUTH CAROLINA, VERMONT
Any person is a mandatory reporter, with exemption for clergy privileged communications (in the reporting law or in the rules of evidence or civil procedure).	DELAWARE, FLORIDA, IDAHO, INDIANA, KENTUCKY, MARYLAND, NEBRASKA, NEW JERSEY, NEW MEXICO, RHODE ISLAND, TEXAS, UTAH, WYOMING	ARIZONA	
Clergy are mandatory reporters, included in another category of mandatory reporters, with exemption for privileged communications.	LOUISIANA, MISSOURI, SOUTH CAROLINA		

Category		
Clergy are mandatory reporters, without exemption.	Mississippi, New Hampshire, West Virginia	Connecticut, Kansas, Kentucky, Maryland, West Virginia
Any person is a mandatory reporter, without exemption.	North Carolina, Oklahoma, Tennessee	Florida, Rhode Island
Clergy reporting not addressed (but clergy may have privilege in other parts of state statutes).	Alabama, Alaska, Arkansas, Colorado, District of Columbia, Georgia, Hawaii, Illinois, Iowa, Kansas, Massachusetts, Michigan, New York, Ohio, South Dakota, Vermont, Virginia, Wisconsin	

Sources: Categories and information in columns 1–2 are adapted from the National Clearinghouse on Child Abuse and Neglect Information's *Reporting Laws: Mandatory Reporters of Child Abuse and Neglect* (Washington, D.C.: Department of Health and Human Services, 2002). Information in columns 3–5 is based on my research, through 9 May 2003.

Index

About the Author

David Yamane teaches sociology at Wake Forest University. He is author of *Student Movements for Multiculturalism: Challenging the Curricular Color Line in Higher Education* (Johns Hopkins University Press, 2001), co-author with Sarah MacMillen and Kelly Culver of *Real Stories of Christian Initiation: Lessons for and from the RCIA* (The Liturgical Press, 2006), and editor of *Goodbye Father: The Celibate Male Priesthood and the Future of the Catholic Church* by Richard Schoenherr (Oxford University Press, 2002). He also edits the professional journal, *Sociology of Religion: A Quarterly Review*. David lives in Winston-Salem, North Carolina with his wife, Megan Polzer, and three children, Paul, Hannah, and Mark.